SEWING FOR CHILDREN

Stylish clothes for every occasion

100 IDÉES
CONRAN OCTOPUS

Originally published as CHILDREN'S CLOTHES in 1986 by
Conran Octopus Limited
37 Shelton Street
London WC2H 9HN

Reprinted in 1988

This revised edition published in 1991

The editors would like to thank Chris Jefferys and
Jeanette Simpson for their assistance.

British Library Cataloguing in Publication Data
Sewing for children: stylish clothes for every occasion.
   1. Children's clothing. Sewing
   I. 100 Idées
   646.406

ISBN 1 85029 321 X

Typeset by SX Composing Limited

Printed and bound in Hong Kong

CONTENTS

THE BASIC ESSENTIALS   6

BABY BLUE BLOOMERS *for a day at the seaside*   8

JAPANESE STYLE *flower power to keep out the chill*   11

FANCY JUMPSUIT *cuddly outfit for baby's first steps*   14

ALL-IN-ONE SUITS *for indoors and outdoors*   18

BORN IN AN ORCHARD *the pick of the bunch*   22

BEDTIME FUN *sleepy clothes for evenings at home*   26

ONE YEAR OLD ALREADY *chintz and ribbons for a star turn* 34

GOOD MORNING *wooden toys to wake up with*   36

TUTTI FRUTTI *in four fabulous flavours*   38

SMART STEPHANIE *tailored pleats for summer chic*   42

SHIPMATES *for fair-weather friends*   43

LIKE A FEATHER IN THE WIND *ballerinas Degas-style*   46

GALA TEA *a special frock for a grand event*   50

FULL SPEED AHEAD *for the sportsman on the move*   55

PLASTIC PRACTICALITY *for rainy day appointments*   58

PATCHWORK PARKAS *bold colours to beat winter glooms*   60

THE SQUARE BAND *cosy comfort for small lumberjacks*   66

PARTY PURSES *for fashionable ladies*   69

VERSATILE COLLARS *for every occasion*   74

APPLIQUE TRICKS *all creatures great and small*   76

ACKNOWLEDGMENTS   80

INTRODUCTION

Children's clothes are fun to make, and quick too. With these patterns you will be able to create beautiful stylish garments that will stand out from the mass-produced designs to be found in the chain stores, and you can choose colours and fabrics to suit your individual child. There are no hard-and-fast rules to observe when sewing for children, but if you follow a few guide lines you will be more than pleased with the results.

Children love to romp around outdoors, mess about with paints and enjoy exuberant mealtimes, so their clothes must be able to withstand wear-and-tear and lots of washing. Choose easy-wear, easy-care fabrics for every day – cottons and synthetic mixtures are ideal, and they're easy to sew too. Always use a thread that matches the type of fabric you have bought and try to stick to simple fastenings – snap-on press studs, touch-and-close fastenings and self-ties are quick to apply to fabric and are handy for small fingers.

Children adore bright colours, so bear this in mind when shopping for fabric – try the furnishing fabric department for large prints, which are a fun alternative to ginghams and stripes. And as children's clothes don't need much fabric, dressmaking is a great way to use up odd remnants and perhaps, once in a while, indulge in some organdie and lace for a special occasion. Remember, too, that children grow quickly, so lengthen the life of trousers, for example, by making them extra long and simply rolling them up.

In this book you will find clothes for all ages, for indoors and outdoors, for playtime and party time, as well as some amusing novelty bags and appliqué ideas. Each pattern is accompanied by a set of easy-to-follow instructions with detailed diagrams, so you just can't go wrong when making these up-to-the-minute designs.

THE BASIC ESSENTIALS

ENLARGING A GRID PATTERN

The easiest way to enlarge a grid pattern is to use dressmakers' pattern paper, which comes ruled with 1cm (⅜in) squares; darker lines mark out the 5cm (2in) squares. One square on the pattern will equal a given measurement – for example, '1 square = 5cm (2in)'

▥ Select a starting point on the pattern, then mark a corresponding point on the pattern paper. Find the adjacent point on the pattern and mark the same point on the paper. Continue carefully round the pattern, marking out the squares until the complete pattern emerges. Where the lines are straight simply join them up with a ruler. Where the line is curved, plot round the lines and join them up together freehand. Then simply cut out the pattern piece.

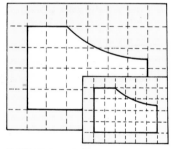

HOW TO ALTER A PAPER PATTERN

▥ All the paper patterns in this book can be altered to fit.
▥ First mark where the patterns can be altered. The bodice length should be altered below the chest line, and the width on a line from the centre of the shoulder to the waist. To alter the skirt mark a line across between the hip and hem for the length, and a line centrally placed from waist to hem for adjusting the width. A sleeve length is altered in equal amounts from above and below the elbow. Mark a central line from top to wrist to change the width. The length of trousers is altered between the crotch and hem, and for the width mark a central line from waist to hem.

▥ Once these adjusting lines have been marked, enlarge the pattern by simply cutting along the marked lines. Move the two halves apart by the required amount and stick a strip of paper behind to join the two halves.
▥ When altering the width of a sleeve head, the armhole size will have to be enlarged. Cut away a small amount from the top of the side edges of both front and back bodice, graduating the new lines back to the original edges.
▥ To reduce a pattern, pin a tuck to remove the required amount along the marked adjusting lines on all the pattern pieces. In some cases the side edges of the pattern will have to be re-drawn to allow for the distortion. If the sleeve head is reduced in size, the armhole edges of both front and back bodice will have to be reduced with the addition of small strips of paper, again graduating the edges back to the original pattern edges.

CUTTING OUT THE PATTERNS

Before you begin it's important to straighten the weft grain of the fabric. Plain woven cottons or cotton blends should be torn, not cut, when you buy them, otherwise, to straighten the ends simply snip into the selvedge and tear across the fabric from one side to the other. On heavier, woven fabrics such as wools or linens, snip into the selvedge and pull out one thread from across the fabric. Cut across the fabric along the marked gap. On jersey use a large set square placed against the selvedge edge and a ruler and simply mark across the fabric.
▥ Fold the fabric in half lengthways with all edges together. If there is distortion, pull the fabric diagonally from corner to corner. Press the fabric to remove any creases.
▥ When the pattern pieces need to be placed against a fabric fold, fold the fabric with the grain lines parallel to the selvedges.
▥ If the fabric has a distinctive pattern or motif, try to position the

main motifs centrally on the main parts of the garments. Where the design has an obvious direction make sure that all pieces of the garment are cut in the same way.
▥ Pin the pattern pieces to the fabric at about 10cm (4in) intervals and cut out with sharp shears. Mark any pocket or button positions before removing the pattern pieces.

WORKING WITH DIFFICULT FABRICS

Jersey
When stitching, use a fine synthetic thread and a ball-point machine needle. Sew with a slight zigzag stitch, which will give a little with the fabric.

Sheer fabrics
When cutting out, pin to a blanket or sheet to prevent the fabric from sliding about the cutting surface. Sew with a fine needle and synthetic thread; if necessary, stitch between layers of tissue paper. Stitch together with French seams and use double hems, to avoid unsightly edges.

Velvet and corduroy
Place the pattern pieces so the pile runs upwards on the finished garment. Stitch together in the direction of the pile, using tissue paper if necessary. Avoid buttonholes; use buttonloops instead or zips, which should be inserted by hand with tiny stitches. When pressing place a piece of self-fabric over or under the fabric to prevent the pile from flattening.

PVC
Hold the pattern pieces in position with adhesive tape. Use the same method when holding pieces together for stitching. When stitching, use a roller foot to help feed the fabric through the machine. Do not press PVC with an iron.

Fur fabrics
Place the pattern pieces on single thickness of fabric, pile side down; cut so that the pile runs down the garment. On jersey-

backed fur fabric stitch with a slight zigzag stitch. After stitching shave the pile from the seam allowances and tease out the pile from the stitched seams.

SEAMS AND STITCHES

Plain seam
Place the two fabric pieces with right sides together, raw edges level; pin and stitch together 1.5cm (⅝in) from the raw edges. Work a few stitches in reverse at each end of the seam to secure the threads.

▥ The simplest method of neatening the seam allowance edges is by zigzag stitching on a machine. Use a short, narrow stitch worked slightly in from the raw edge. If the fabric has a tendency to fray use a larger stitch and work over the raw edge. Where the fabric is fine turn under the raw edge and either zigzag stitch or stitch with a straight stitch. If neatening by hand oversew the raw edges: work from left to right (or vice versa, if you are left-handed), taking the thread diagonally over the edge and keeping the stitches about 3mm (⅛in) apart. If the fabric tends to fray work a row of straight stitching first, then oversew over the edge. If the fabric is heavy simply pink the edges using a pair of pinking shears.

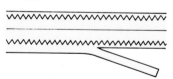

French seam
A self-neatening seam used mainly on sheer and lightweight fabrics. Place the two fabric pieces with wrong sides together; pin and stitch 1cm (⅜in) from the raw edges. Trim and press the seam open. Refold with right sides together; pin and stitch 6mm (¼in) from the seamed edge.

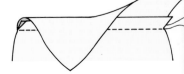

Flat fell seam

A self-neatening seam, which is very strong and distinctive. Place the two pieces with right sides together; pin and stitch a plain seam. Press seam allowance to one side. Trim down the lower seam allowance to 6mm (¼in). Fold the upper seam allowance over, enclosing the lower seam allowance. Press the folded allowance flat against the fabric; pin and stitch close to the folded edge.

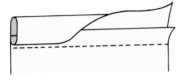

Slipstitching

This hand stitch is used to join two folded edges together – for example, to close an opening.

Bring the needle into one fold and come out 2-3mm (⅛in) further along; take a stitch the same length through the opposite fold. Pull the thread through and repeat. The stitches should be almost invisible.

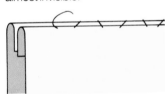

Buttonhole stitch

Work the stitches close together, with the raw edge away from you. Insert the needle through the fabric 6mm (¼in) from the edge over the working thread; when the needle is pulled through a tiny loop is formed at the buttonhole edge. Do not pull the stitches too tight or the edge will pucker.

Topstitching

Stitching worked from the right side of the garment to emphasize the seam. Buttonhole thread can be used to make the stitching heavier and more visible.

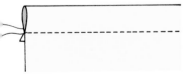

Hemming

Work this stitch with the hem away from you. After securing the working thread under the hem, take a tiny stitch through the main fabric – picking up one or two threads – and then a tiny stitch through the hem, then pull through; repeat, starting the next stitch directly below. The stitches should be about 6mm (¼in) apart.

Running stitch

This is the simplest of all the hand stitches; weave the needle through the fabric at regular, short intervals. The spaces between the stitches are the same size as the stitches themselves. This stitch is most commonly used for gathering up fabrics.

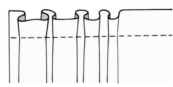

FASTENINGS

How to stitch on a button

At the marked position for the button, secure the thread on the right side of the fabric. Pass the needle through the button; hold a matchstick over the top of the button and work about 10 stitches over it through the holes of the button. Remove the matchstick and pull the button up; wind the working thread around the excess threads underneath button; work two backstitches into this shank and fasten off.

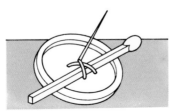

When the button itself has a shank, after securing the thread, take small stitches through the shank, again about 10 times. Fasten off.

How to make a buttonloop

Mark the position of the loop on the fabric. Secure the thread on the wrong side of the fabric at one end of loop position. Bring thread through to right side and take a tiny stitch at the opposite end, leaving a loop of thread the correct size. Take thread back to starting point, leaving a second loop. Make two more loops in the same way and then buttonhole stitch over the loops. Fasten off.

Stitched buttonholes

Tack all round the buttonhole position and then cut along the marked line through all layers. Either using buttonhole thread or an ordinary sewing thread, secure the thread and begin at the inside edge of the garment. Work along the slit in buttonhole stitch, fanning out the stitches at the outside edge. Continue along the opposite side and then work a straight bar of stitches on the inside edge. Fasten off.

When working vertical buttonholes, work a bar at both ends.

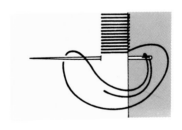

Press stud fasteners

There are several types of clamp-on studs and eyelets available; they are usually sold with the special tool for fixing them in place. In each case there are two parts to each section, which are fastened in place on either side of the fabric. Plain or decorative heads are available.

As an alternative to press fasteners, there are touch-and-close spots – small discs of nylon hooks and loops that cling together when pressed. Stitch these discs in place with a triangle of stitching.

How to stitch on a press fastener

Separate the two halves – the flatter half of the fastener will be sewn to the overlapping fabric, the curved socket to the underlap.

Position the top half to the fabric, at least 3mm (⅛in) from the edge. Secure the thread and work five or six stitches in each hole of the fastener, taking the needle under the fastener to the next hole each time. Fasten off the thread. Mark the position of the opposite half and stitch in place in the same way.

How to stitch on hooks and eyes

Stitch the hook to the overlapping fabric and the eye or bar to the underneath. After securing the thread, hold the hook firmly and work five to six stitches round the first loop, take the needle through the fabric to the next loop and repeat; then take the needle through the fabric to the end of the hook and work several stitches over the hook. Fasten off the thread. Stitch the eye or bar in place by stitching through the loops in the same way.

How to insert a zip

Pin and stitch the seam up to the zip opening, then tack the remainder of the seam. Press the seam open. Place the zip face downwards over the seam allowances with the bottom stop 3mm (⅛in) below the beginning of the tacking and the teeth centred over the tacked seam. Tack in place through all layers 6mm (¼in) on either side of the teeth. Turn to the right side. Stitch the zip in place using a zipper foot on the machine, following tacking lines at the sides, and pivoting the stitching at the bottom corners.

BABY BLUE BLOOMERS

A nautical stripe gives these beach bloomers great style. Elastic threaded at waist and ankle keeps sand and dirt out and they are stitched with French seams for a firm, tidy finish. The little shirt matches in spick-and-span fine stripes. Choose a soft, light seersucker fabric for coolness.

Size: to fit a one-year-old baby.

MATERIALS

BLOOMERS	SHIRT
50cm (⅝yd) of 90cm (36in) wide seersucker	*1m (1yd) of 90cm (36in) wide seersucker*
50cm (⅝yd) of 2.5cm (1in) wide elastic	*60cm (¾yd) of 2.5cm (1in) wide self-fabric binding cut on the fabric bias*
50cm (⅝yd) of 1cm (⅜in) wide elastic	*Four 1.5cm (⅝in) diameter buttons*
Two 1.5cm (⅝in) diameter buttons	*Dressmakers' pattern paper*
Dressmakers' pattern paper	*Matching thread*
Matching thread	

METHOD FOR BLOOMERS

▦ Draw up patterns from diagrams. Cut out following cutting instructions.

▦ Place fronts together; pin and stitch centre front with French seam. Repeat with backs. Place front to back; pin and stitch sides and inner legs with French seams.

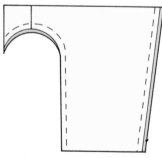

▦ Pin and stitch short ends of waistband together to form a ring. Place one edge of waistband to bloomer top with right sides together; pin and stitch. Fold waistband in half, then turn under remaining raw edge; pin and stitch, leaving an opening at centre back seam.

▦ Thread wider elastic through the waistband; overlap ends for 1cm (⅜in) and stitch together. Push elastic into waistband and

stitch up opening. Work two rows of stitching around the waistband over the elastic, evenly spacing rows about 6mm (¼in) apart.

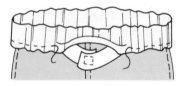

▦ Fold each strap in half lengthways with right sides together; pin and stitch the long side, leaving a central opening. Refold with seam to centre and stitch across both ends. Trim and turn to right side; slipstitch central opening to close.

▦ Place straps to right side of trouser back 3cm (1¼in) from centre back seam; pin and stitch in place. Work two vertical buttonholes on opposite ends of straps. Sew two buttons to inside of the waistband on either side of centre front.

▦ Turn up a 1.5cm (⅝in) casing hem at the base of each leg, then tuck under 6mm (¼in); pin and stitch, leaving an opening at a seam. Stitch all around lower edge of hem. Thread elastic through casing; overlap ends for 1cm (⅜in) and stitch together. Push elastic into casing and stitch up opening.

for *a day at the seaside*

METHOD FOR SHIRT

▦ Draw up patterns from diagrams. Cut out following cutting instructions.

▦ Place backs to front; pin and stitch together at shoulders and sides with French seams.

▦ Fold sleeves in half; pin and stitch with French seams. Pin sleeves in armholes, matching side seams; stitch with French seams. Turn up a double 3cm (1¼in) hem along base of each sleeve; pin and stitch.

▦ Turn in centre back edges along marked line. Open out one folded edge of bias binding and, with right sides together, place along seamline of neck edge; pin and stitch along fold line of binding. Press binding to the inside; pin and slipstitch in place.

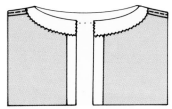

▦ Turn up lower edge of shirt for 2.5cm (1in), then tuck under 6mm (¼in); pin and hem.

▦ Work four horizontal buttonholes evenly spaced down right back, placing top buttonhole at neck edge. Stitch buttons to left back to correspond with buttonholes.

9

BABY BLUE BLOOMERS

Pattern for bloomers

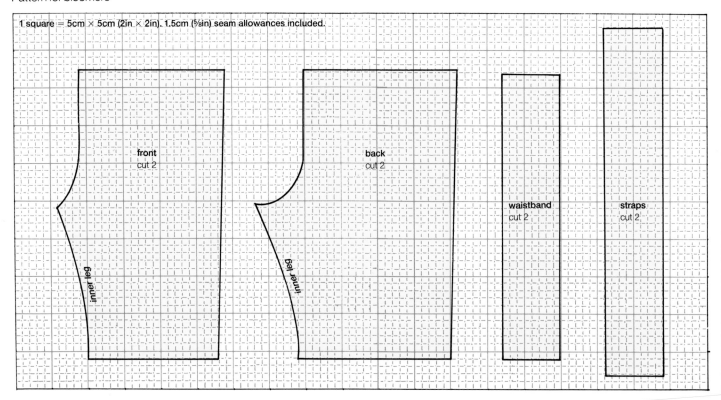

1 square = 5cm × 5cm (2in × 2in). 1.5cm (⅝in) seam allowances included.

front
cut 2

inner leg

back
cut 2

inner leg

waistband
cut 2

straps
cut 2

Pattern for shirt

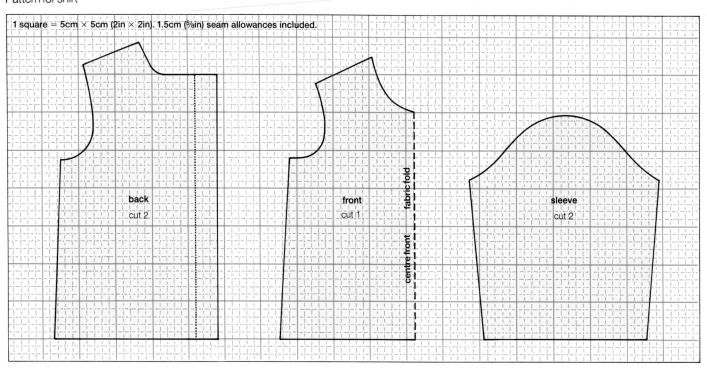

1 square = 5cm × 5cm (2in × 2in). 1.5cm (⅝in) seam allowances included.

back
cut 2

front
cut 1

centre front

fabric fold

sleeve
cut 2

JAPANESE STYLE

High-fashion 'pareo' fabric makes a kimono-style jacket that fits easily over a wool jumper. The jacket is padded to keep baby snug and lined in a firm striped fabric to match the little trousers. Cut out the kimono front and back with a big splash of flower in the centre of the panels for the best decorative effect.

Size: to fit a nine-month-old baby.

MATERIALS

For jacket and trousers.
1.2m (1¼yd) of 90cm (36in) wide large floral cotton fabric
2m (2⅛yd) of 90cm (36in) wide striped cotton fabric

70cm (¾yd) of 90cm (36in) wide 114gm (4oz) wadding
40cm (½yd) of 1.2cm (½in) wide elastic
Six press studs

METHOD FOR JACKET

▦ Draw up patterns from diagrams. Cut out following cutting instructions. Stripes should run around jacket.

▦ Tack wadding to wrong side of floral fabric. Pin and stich floral jacket together at shoulder and side/underarm seams.

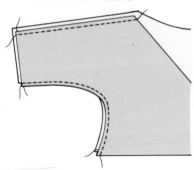

▦ With right sides together, stitch facing to neckline of striped jacket back. Trim turnings. Clip curve. Press facing up. Stitch on wadding facing (do not press).

▦ Stitch striped jacket together at side/underarm seams and shoulder seams, continuing stitching across facings.

▦ With right sides together place floral jacket to striped jacket; pin and stitch left front edges from A round the base to right front at B. Trim and turn to right side. Topstitch round the outline of the larger flowers, working through all three layers.

▦ Place collar facing over edge of floral jacket, turn under seam allowance; pin and topstitch in place, trimming away excess wadding if necessary.

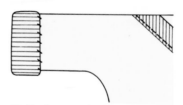

▦ Turn sleeve facing on to floral side of jacket, turn under seam allowance; pin and hem in place by hand.

▦ For ties, cut six pieces of striped fabric on the straight, 26cm × 2.5cm (10¼in × 1in).

▦ Fold ties in half lengthways with right sides together; pin and stitch across one end and down length, taking a 6mm (¼in) seam allowance. Trim and turn to right side. Turn in raw edges at open end; slipstitch to close.

▦ Handstitch ties to floral side of jacket at B, C, D, E and F, and to striped side of jacket at G.

METHOD FOR TROUSERS

▦ Place trousers with right sides together; pin and stitch centre seams.

▦ Turn down 2cm (¾in) at top edge, then tuck under 6mm(¼in). Pin and stitch in place close to hem edge leaving an opening at one seam. Work a second line of stitching close to top edge of trousers.

▦ Insert elastic round waist; overlap ends for 1cm (⅜in) and stitch together. Push elastic into waistband and stitch up opening.

▦ Turn a narrow double hem round inner leg seams. Fix press stud fasteners in place, evenly spaced round the opening.

▦ Turn up hem on base of each trouser leg for 2.5cm (1in), then tuck under 6mm (¼in); pin and hem in place by hand.

The large flowers on the cross-over jacket are emphasized with topstitching and team up with press-stud-closed trousers.

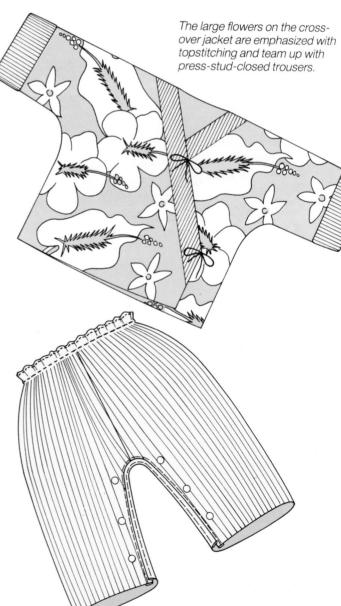

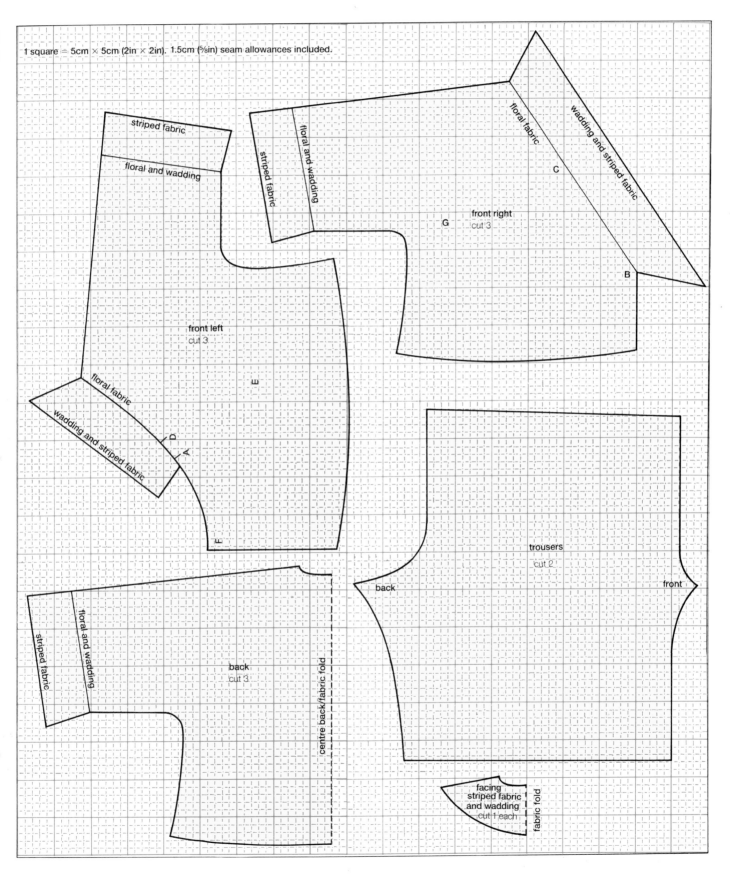

1 square = 5cm × 5cm (2in × 2in). 1.5cm (⅝in) seam allowances included.

striped fabric

floral and wadding

striped fabric

floral and wadding

floral fabric

wadding and striped fabric

C

front right
cut 3

G

B

front left
cut 3

E

floral fabric

wadding and striped fabric

D

A

F

trousers
cut 2

back

front

striped fabric

floral and wadding

back
cut 3

centre back/fabric fold

facing
striped fabric
and wadding
cut 1 each

fabric fold

FANCY JUMPSUIT

There's no need for jumpsuits to be utilitarian gro-bags – make a feature of their loose fit with a design reminiscent of a clown's jumpsuit. The pretty stepped cut-out is easy to sew and simply fastened in place with touch-and-close spots. Use contrast colours with all the magic of the ring: red and yellow, blue and white, green and sizzling pink.

Size: to fit an eighteen-month-old baby

MATERIALS

80cm (⅞yd) of 140cm (55in) wide red brushed jersey
40cm (½yd) of 140cm (55in) wide yellow brushed jersey
Two sets of stretch cuffs: one red, one yellow

Two stretch waistbands: one red, one yellow
Touch-and-close spots
Dressmakers' pattern paper
Matching thread

METHOD

◫ Draw up patterns from diagrams. Cut out following cutting instructions.
◫ Place red backs with right sides together; pin and stitch centre back seam.
◫ Fold under seam allowance on yellow back, then place over seam allowance on red back; pin and topstitch in place.

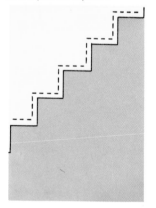

◫ Place the red fronts with right sides together; pin and stitch centre front seam. Place facing to red front with right sides together; pin and stitch. Snip corners. Turn facing to inside and topstitch. Neaten base edge of facing. Stitch touch-and-close spots to facing.
◫ Neaten lower edge of yellow front upper left section. Stitch opposite halves of touch-and-close spots to yellow front section to correspond with those on red facing.

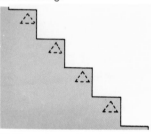

◫ Place sleeves in pairs with right sides together; pin and stitch centre seams. Position sleeves to body sections; pin and stitch in place.
◫ Pin and stitch side seams from wrist along underarm seams to ankles, catching edges of facings in the seam.
◫ With right sides together, stitch stretch cuffs to sleeve bases, slightly stretching the ribbed cuff as you sew. Repeat for ankle bands.

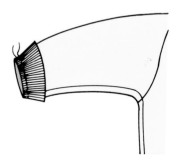

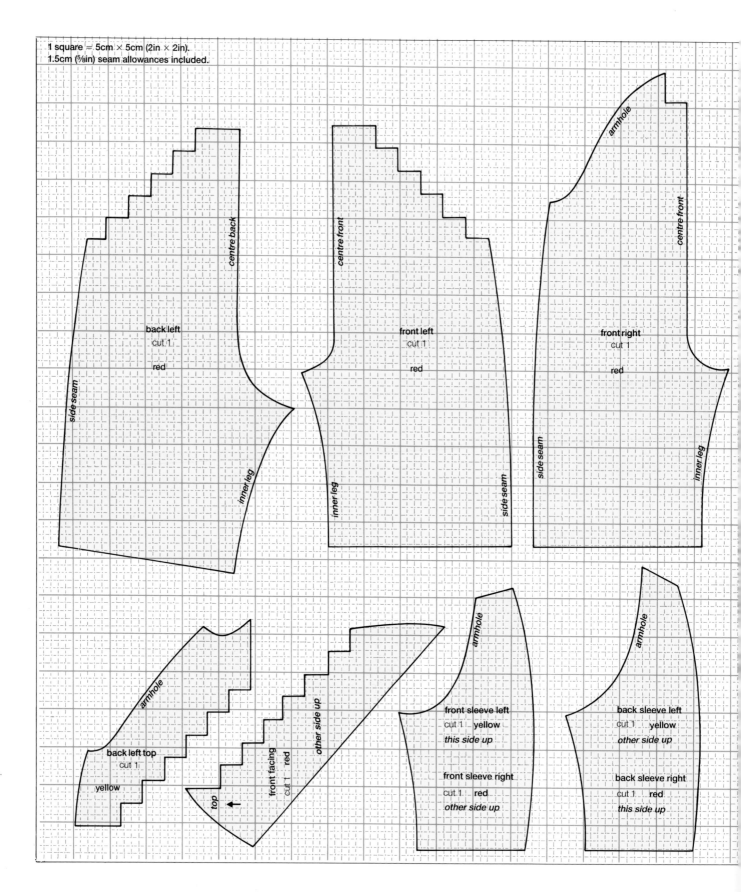

1 square = 5cm × 5cm (2in × 2in).
1.5cm (⅝in) seam allowances included.

back left
cut 1
red

centre back

side seam

inner leg

front left
cut 1
red

centre front

inner leg

front right
cut 1
red

centre front

armhole

side seam

inner leg

back left top
cut 1
yellow

armhole

front facing
cut 1   red

top

other side up

front sleeve left
cut 1   yellow
this side up

armhole

front sleeve right
cut 1   red
other side up

back sleeve left
cut 1   yellow
other side up

armhole

back sleeve right
cut 1   red
this side up

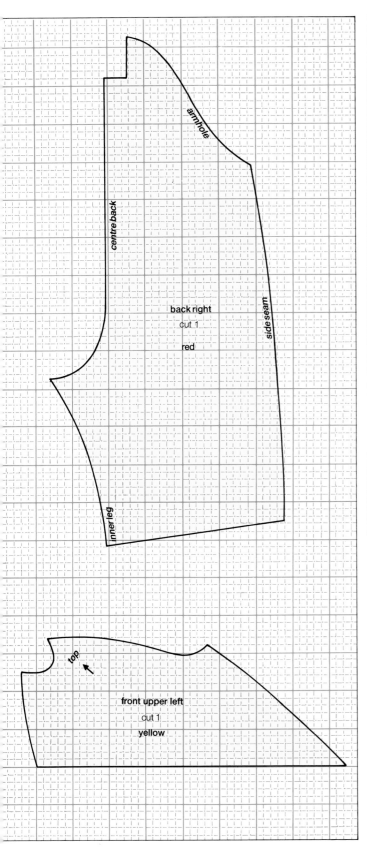

centre back

armhole

side seam

back right

cut 1

red

inner leg

top

front upper left

cut 1

yellow

▦ For collar cut one piece from red waistband 9cm × 8cm (3½in × 3¼in) for right collar, and one piece from yellow waistband 23cm × 8cm (9in × 3¼in) for left collar.

▦ With right sides together, pin and stitch collars together. Fold collar in half lengthways with right sides together; pin and stitch ends. Turn to right side and stitch to neck edge, slightly stretching as you sew. Fasten at neck with one touch-and-close spot.

The zigzagged front hides a row of touch-and-close spots, while the wrists and ankles are finished with stretch fabric bands.

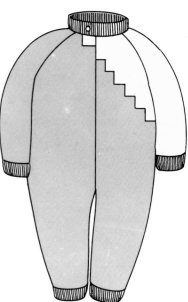

ALL-IN-ONE SUITS

But forget the workaday overall image – these new designs are much more fun and they are ideal for all sorts of activities.

Make the indoor version in a glowing chintzy cotton that is irresistible for lounging in or can be worn at bedtime in place of a dowdy old dressing gown. The outdoor version in a windproof fabric will fit over the chunkiest knit, and has big patch pockets to hide little secrets. Elasticated wrists and a strong front zip keep wet and wind out.

Size: to fit a two-year-old.

MATERIALS

1.5m (1⅝yd) of 112/114cm (45in) wide plain or printed cotton fabric	30cm (12in) of elastic Dressmakers' pattern paper Matching thread
30cm(12in) zip (outdoor suit)	

METHOD

▨ Draw up patterns from diagrams. Cut out following cutting instructions.

▨ Place backs with right sides together; pin and stitch centre back seam. Repeat with front pieces, but only stitch seam from A to B. Neaten. Turn in seam allowance on either side of centre front from A to neck edge; tack.

▨ Turn in 6mm (¼in) on top edge of each pocket; pin and stitch. Turn down the right side of each pocket top for 2cm (¾in); pin and stitch sides. Snip corners and turn facing to inside of pocket; topstitch across top edge. Turn under seam allowance all round outer edge of pocket; tack. Place pockets on fronts at marked positions; pin and topstitch.

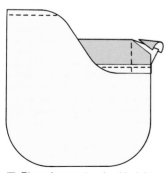

▨ Place front to back with right sides together; pin and stitch

shoulder, side and inner leg seams. Neaten. Turn up 2.5cm (1in) hem at base of each leg, then tuck under 6mm (¼in); pin and stitch hem.

▨ Fold sleeves in half with right sides together; pin and stitch seams. Pin sleeves in armholes with right sides together, matching underarm seams; stitch. Neaten.

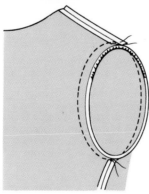

▨ At the base of each sleeve either turn up a 2.5cm (1in) hem then tuck under 6mm (¼in); pin and stitch hem.

▨ Or, for a gathered sleeve, pin and stitch, leaving an opening at seam. Using a safety pin, thread elastic through the casing from opening in the seam; overlap ends of elastic for 1cm (⅜in) and stitch together firmly. Push elastic into casing and stitch up opening by hand or machine.

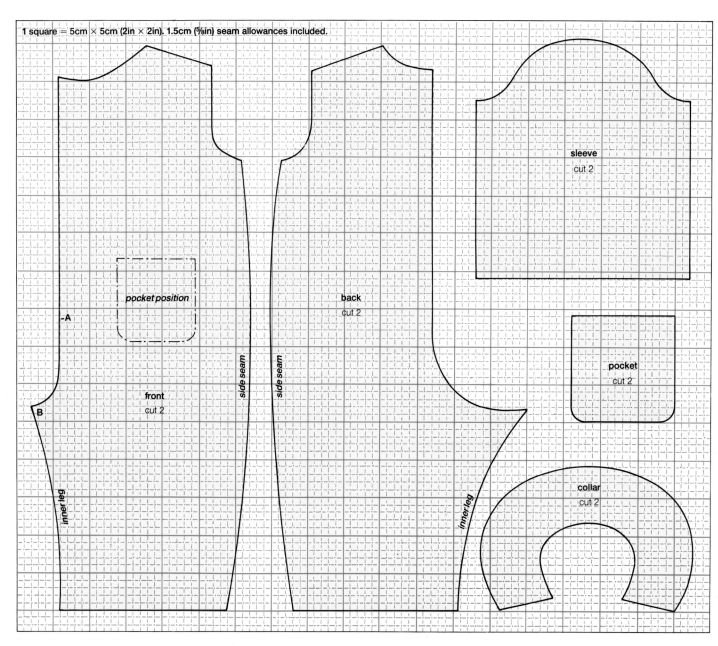

1 square = 5cm × 5cm (2in × 2in). 1.5cm (⅝in) seam allowances included.

sleeve
cut 2

pocket position

-A

back
cut 2

side seam

side seam

pocket
cut 2

front
cut 2

B

inner leg

inner leg

collar
cut 2

▦ If closing the centre front with a zip, insert now, before adding the collar.

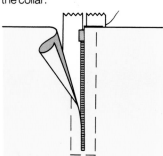

▦ Place collars with right sides together; pin and stitch all round outer edge, leaving neck edge open. Trim and turn to right side.
▦ Place one neck edge of collar to neck edge of suit with right sides together, matching collar edges to folded front edges; pin and stitch.

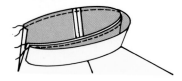

▦ Turn under remaining raw edge and slipstitch over previous stitches. Topstitch around collar, 6mm (¼in) from outer edge.
▦ If closing the centre front with ties, make up four pairs of 20cm × 1cm (8in × ⅜in) long ties: cut eight pieces of fabric on the bias, each 21cm × 3.5cm (8¼in × 1¼in). Fold each in half lengthways with right sides together; pin and stitch across one end and down the length taking 6mm (¼in) seam allowance. Trim and turn to right

side. Turn in raw edges and sew on in pairs evenly spaced from neck edge down the centre.

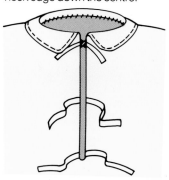

Outdoors, a neat zip fastens this all-in-one suit against the cold, while indoors self-fabric ties are the chintzy answer.

BORN IN AN ORCHARD

On hot summer days, little kids need comfy and loosely fitting clothes for running about. These clever playsuits are roomy with eye-catching detail at the shoulders. For delectable little girls and boys, make strawberry trims for the trouser shoulder straps, and sweet cherry ties on the sleeved suit. Note the French perfection of tucks on the cuffs to match the fronts – that's summer chic!

Sizes: to fit a two-year-old.

MATERIALS

PYJAMAS
1.7m (1⅞yd) of 90cm (36in) wide green poplin
1.5m (1⅝yd) of 2.5cm (1in) wide red bias binding
Dressmakers' pattern paper
Fabric for 4 strawberry motifs
Matching thread

COMBINATION SUIT
2m (2⅛yd) of 90cm (36in) wide acid green or pink poplin
2m (2⅛yd) of 2.5cm (1in) wide bias binding, in contrasting colour
1.2m (1⅜yd) of 1.3cm (½in) wide bias binding
Dressmakers' pattern paper
Fabric for 8 cherry motifs
Matching thread

METHOD FOR MOTIFS

STRAWBERRIES
▨ Cut out two strawberry shapes from fabric.
▨ Using ecru embroidery cotton, work a few evenly spaced running stitches on the right side of each shape for seeds.
▨ Place with right sides together; pin and stitch together close to outer edge, leaving a small opening at the top. Turn to right side. Fill with suitable filling and stitch up opening.
▨ Cut out two leaves from fabric in different shades of green. Fix one leaf on top of the other.

CHERRIES
▨ Cut out a 6.5cm (2½in) diameter circle from fabric.
▨ Turn in a narrow hem all round the edge. Work a gathering stitch close to hemmed outer edge. Fill with suitable filling. Pull up gathering thread around filling and fasten off.

METHOD FOR PYJAMAS

▦ Draw up pattern from diagram. Cut out following cutting instructions.

▦ Place back/front pieces with right sides together; pin and stitch centre front and then centre back seams, leaving 7cm (2¾in) open at top.

▦ Fold and pin eight 2cm (¾in) wide knife pleats along the top front so they face away from centre front, as shown in diagram. Fold and pin four 2cm (¾in) wide knife pleats along each back section in the same way. Using red thread, topstitch down the fold edge of each pleat for 6cm (2½in).

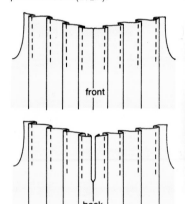

▦ Fold and pin eight 2cm (¾in) wide knife pleats around the base of each leg; topstitch up the fold edge of each pleat for 8cm (3¼in). Stitch inner leg seam.

▦ Open out one folded edge of bias binding and, with right sides together, place along back opening; pin and stitch along fold line of binding. Press binding to the inside; pin and stitch in place.

▦ Fold bias binding in half lengthways over raw edges of armholes, legs and neck edges, turning under raw edges at back opening; pin and stitch in place.

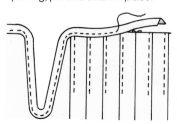

▦ Make up four ties each 20cm × 1cm (8in × ⅜in): cut four pieces of fabric on the bias, each 21cm × 3.5cm (8¼in × 1¼in). Fold each in half lengthways with right sides together; pin and stitch across one end and down the length, taking a 6mm (¼in) seam allowance. Trim and turn to right side. Turn in raw edges at open end and slipstitch, then place, inside the garment, in pairs at the end of the outer front and back pleats; pin and handstitch in place. Stitch a strawberry motif to the end of each tie.

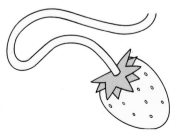

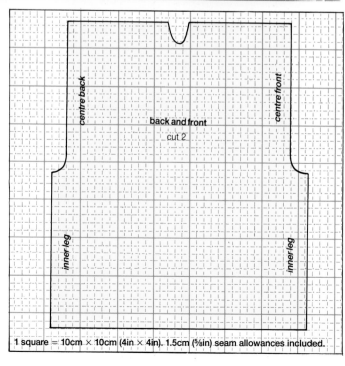

centre back

centre front

back and front
cut 2

inner leg

inner leg

1 square = 10cm × 10cm (4in × 4in). 1.5cm (⅝in) seam allowances included.

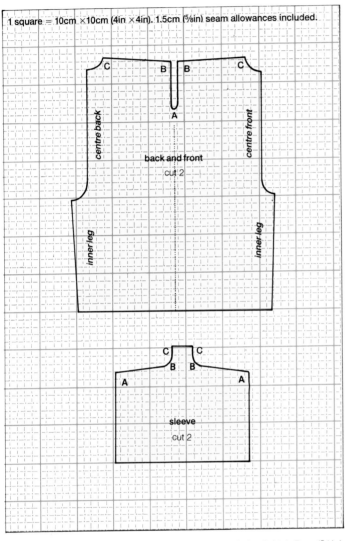

1 square = 10cm ×10cm (4in ×4in). 1.5cm (⅝in) seam allowances included.

centre back

centre front

C — B — B — C

A

back and front
cut 2

inner leg

inner leg

C — C
B — B
A — A

sleeve
cut 2

METHOD FOR COMBINATION SUIT

▦ Draw up patterns from diagrams. Cut out following cutting instructions.
▦ Fold and pin four 1.5cm (⅝in) wide knife pleats on each back and front shoulder, as shown in the diagram. Using contrasting thread, topstitch down the fold edge of each pleat for 6cm (2½in).

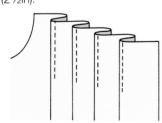

▦ Fold and pin eight 1.5cm (⅝in) wide knife pleats around the base of each sleeve. Using contrasting thread, topstitch up the fold edge of each pleat for 4cm (1½in).
▦ Fold and pin eight 2cm (¾in) wide knife pleats around the base of each leg. Using contrasting thread, topstitch up the fold edge of each pleat for 6cm (2½in).
▦ Place back/front pieces with right sides together; pin and stitch centre back and then centre front seam for 8cm (3¼in). Pin and stitch inner leg seams.
▦ Fold sleeves in half with right sides together; pin and stitch seams. Pin sleeves in armholes with right sides together, matching the As, Bs and Cs; stitch. Press the seams flat towards the sleeve; topstitch

seams in contrasting thread.

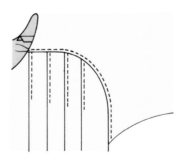

▦ Bind the centre front opening, sleeves, legs and neck edge with bias binding in the same way as for the pyjamas.
▦ For the ties, cut eight 15cm (6in) lengths from 1.3cm (½in)

wide binding. Fold in half lengthways; pin and stitch down length, then tuck in raw edges at each end. Stitch ties in pairs behind front opening, spacing them 9cm (3½in) apart, with top pair at neck edge. Stitch a cherry motif to the end of each tie.

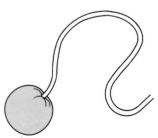

BEDTIME FUN

Three stunning outfits in cuddly brushed cotton give you sing-song colours and easy-to-sew shapes. There's a design to please every personality: 'Jump for Joy', a sleepsuit with a pierrot collar for the irrepressible; 'Yellow Delight', a mini-dressing gown for the man about the house, and 'Red at Night', a glamour gown with a hood and pompons. Don't forget the Mr. Mouse bootees, which will be a joy to all parties.

Sizes: to fit a two-year-old.

MATERIALS

BOOTEES
10cm (4in) of 90cm (36in) wide brushed cotton
50cm (20in) of bias binding in a matching colour
15cm (6in) square of non-slip material
Fabric adhesive

One 50g (2oz) ball of Pingouin Fine+
Pair of 2¾mm (size 12) knitting needles
Two mother-of-pearl buttons, for eyes
Black embroidery cotton, for features
Matching thread

YELLOW DELIGHT
1.4m (1½yd) of 90cm (36in) wide brushed cotton

1m (1yd) of cord in contrasting colour
Matching thread

RED AT NIGHT
1.1m (1⅛yd) of 90cm (36in) wide brushed cotton
3m (3¼yd) of 2cm (¾in) wide braid

Matching thread
Oddments of yarn in three colours

JUMP FOR JOY
1.6m (1¾yd) of 90cm (36in) wide blue brushed cotton
40cm (½yd) of 90cm (36in) wide pink brushed cotton
Oddment of 1.3cm (½in) wide elastic
Two small buttons

1m (1yd) of 1.3cm (½in) wide bias binding
Small amount of filling
Matching thread
One 50g (2oz) ball of Pingouin France +
Pair of 3¾mm (size 9) knitting needles

HOW TO MAKE A POMPON
Cut two circles of cardboard to the required diameter of the pompon. Cut a small circle from the centre of each one. Place the discs together and wind yarn round and round them. When the centre gets full, thread the yarn on to a bodkin and 'sew' through the hole until it is filled. Cut through the loops at the outer edge and pull the pieces of card slightly apart. Tie a short length of yarn firmly round the loops between the two discs. Then pull the discs away and fluff out the finished pompon.

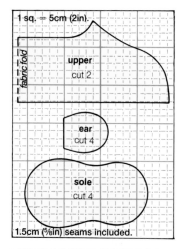

1 sq. = 5cm (2in).

fabric fold

upper
cut 2

ear
cut 4

sole
cut 4

1.5cm (⅝in) seams included.

METHOD FOR BOOTEES

▨ Draw up patterns from diagrams. Cut out following cutting instructions.

▨ Place soles together in pairs with wrong sides together, matching outer edges; pin and zigzag stitch together all round.

▨ Fold each upper in half with right sides together; pin and stitch centre front seam. Place each upper to a combined sole with wrong sides down, matching centre front seam to sole front and centre back fold to sole back; pin and zigzag stitch together all round.

▨ Fold bias binding in half lengthways over zigzagged edges of sole. Turn under raw edge of binding and overlap at centre back to finish; pin and stitch binding in place.

▨ Place the bootee on the wrong side of the non-slip material and mark round it. Cut out two soles; stick to fabric soles. When the adhesive is dry, stitch around bootees again over bias binding.

▨ Place ears together in pairs with right sides together; pin and stitch together all round, leaving base edge open. Trim and turn to right side.

▨ Make a face on each bootee with ears and button eyes, and add a nose in satin stitch and whiskers in long straight stitch.

▨ For each ankle band, cast on 60sts. Work in K1, P1 rib for 10cm (4in). Cast off. Fold in half and stitch seam. Stitch ankle band to top of bootee.

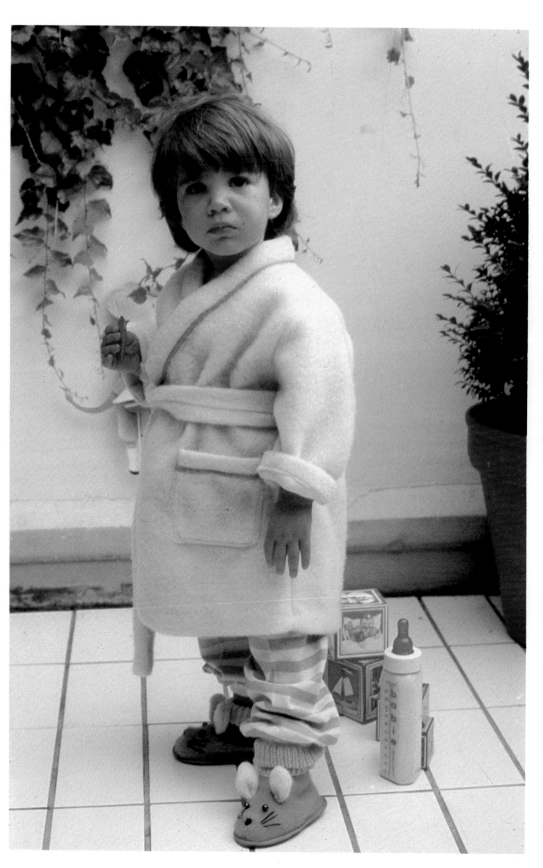

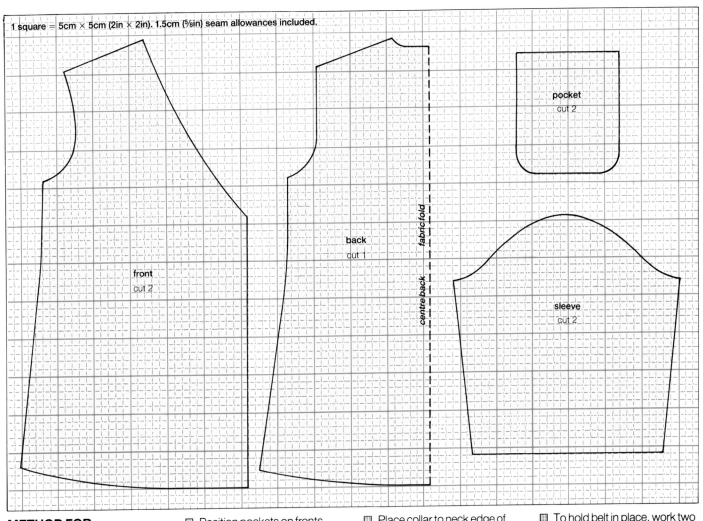

1 square = 5cm × 5cm (2in × 2in). 1.5cm (⅝in) seam allowances included.

pocket
cut 2

back
cut 1

centre back fabricfold

front
cut 2

sleeve
cut 2

METHOD FOR YELLOW DELIGHT

▦ Draw up patterns from diagrams. Cut out following cutting instructions.

▦ From remaining fabric, cut out one collar strip 65cm × 7.5cm (26in × 3in) and one belt strip 140cm × 10cm (54in × 4in).

▦ With right sides together, pin and stitch fronts to back along side and shoulder seams.

▦ To make pocket facing, turn down right side of each pocket top for 2.5cm (1in); pin and stitch sides of facing. Snip corners and turn facing to wrong side of pocket; topstitch across pocket top 2cm (¾in) from edge.

▦ Handstitch cord across topstitching. Turn under remaining edges of pocket; pin and tack.

▦ Position pockets on fronts 6cm (2½in) from side seams and 20cm (8in) up from base edge; pin and topstitch in place.

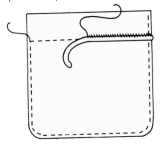

▦ Fold sleeves in half with right sides together; pin and stitch underarm seams.

▦ Pin sleeves in armholes with right sides together, matching centre top of sleeve to shoulder seam and matching underarm seams together; stitch in place.

▦ Place collar to neck edge of dressing gown with right sides together; pin and stitch.

▦ Fold collar in half lengthways with right sides together, overlapping long raw edge by 1.5cm (⅝in); pin and stitch ends. Neaten remaining raw edge; turn; stitch along seamline. Handstitch cord to dressing gown over seamline of collar on right side.

▦ Fold belt in half with right sides together; pin and stitch, leaving a central opening in long side. Trim and turn to right side; slipstitch central opening to close.

▦ To hold belt in place, work two loops slightly larger than belt width at each side seam.

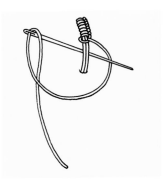

▦ Turn under 6cm (2½in) along base edge, then tuck under 6mm (¼in); pin and hem in place.

▦ Turn under 2.5cm (1in) along lower edge of each sleeve, then tuck under 6mm (¼in); pin and hem in place.

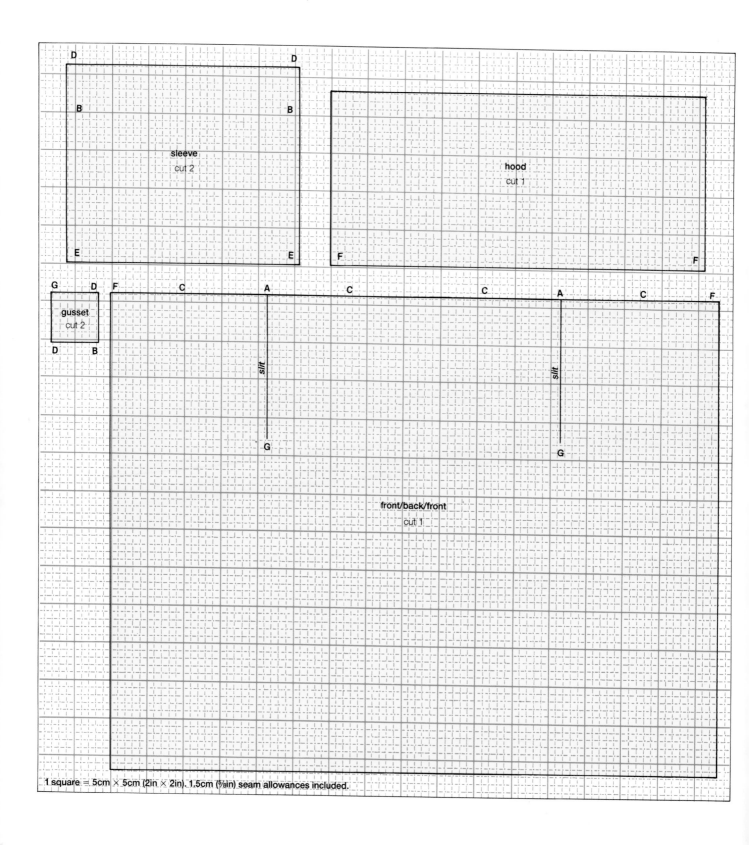

D   D

B   B

sleeve
cut 2

E   E

hood
cut 1

F   F

G   D   F   C   A   C   C   A   C   F

gusset
cut 2

D   B

slit   *slit*

G   G

front/back/front
cut 1

1 square = 5cm × 5cm (2in × 2in). 1.5cm (⅝in) seam allowances included.

METHOD FOR RED AT NIGHT

▦ Draw up patterns from diagrams. Cut out following cutting instructions.

▦ To form armholes cut slits down the combined front/back from A to G for 19.5cm (7½in).

▦ Fold back and front with right sides together; pin and stitch shoulder seams between A and C

▦ Fold sleeve with right sides together and E's and B's matching. Stitch between E and B to make underarm sleeve seam.

▦ Stitch one edge of gusset to one edge of open part of sleeve seam between D and B. Stitch adjacent edge of gusset to other open edge of sleeve between D and B.

▦ Stitch sleeve and gusset to armhole slit, matching G on gusset with G at bottom of slit.

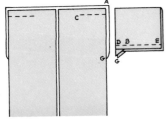

▦ Fold hood in half widthwise with F's matching and stitch centre back seam.

▦ With right sides together, pin and stitch hood to neck edge. Trim and press seam open. Position braid centrally over seam on wrong side covering raw edges; pin and topstitch in place.

▦ Fold braid in half lengthways over raw front edges; pin and topstitch in place. Overlap front braids and stitch centre front seam, leaving 15cm (6in) open at both top and bottom of seam.

▦ Turn under 6cm (2½in) along base edge, then tuck under 6mm (¼in); pin and hem in place. Repeat for each sleeve, but make a 2.5cm (1in) hem.

▦ Make up a pompon from each yarn colour; stitch pompons in place down centre front seam.

METHOD FOR JUMP FOR JOY

▦ Draw up patterns from diagrams. Cut out following cutting instructions.

▦ From remaining pink fabric, cut out two 5cm (2in) diameter circles for pompons.

▦ With right sides together, place lower back to front, pin and stitch side seams from E to D. Neaten side seams and top edge of flap.

▦ Place upper back to front with right sides together, overlapping lower back piece; pin and stitch side seam from D to C.

▦ Turn a 1.5cm (⅝in) hem along side edges of back flap; pin and stitch. Turn under a 2cm (¾in) hem along top edge of back flap; pin and stitch. Push a length of elastic through back casing and stitch at each end to hold. Work a horizontal buttonhole at each end of back casing.

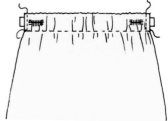

▦ Work a tight zigzag stitch around curved edge of upper back. Stitch a button to edges of upper back to match buttonholes.

▦ Cut a 10cm (4in) slit at centre back neck and neaten edges with bias binding.

▦ With right sides together, pin and stitch inner leg seams.

▦ Fold sleeve in half with right sides together; pin and stitch sleeve seams. Pin sleeves in armholes with right sides together, matching AC and BC; stitch in place.

▦ Work buttonhole stitch all round outer edge of collar.

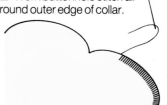

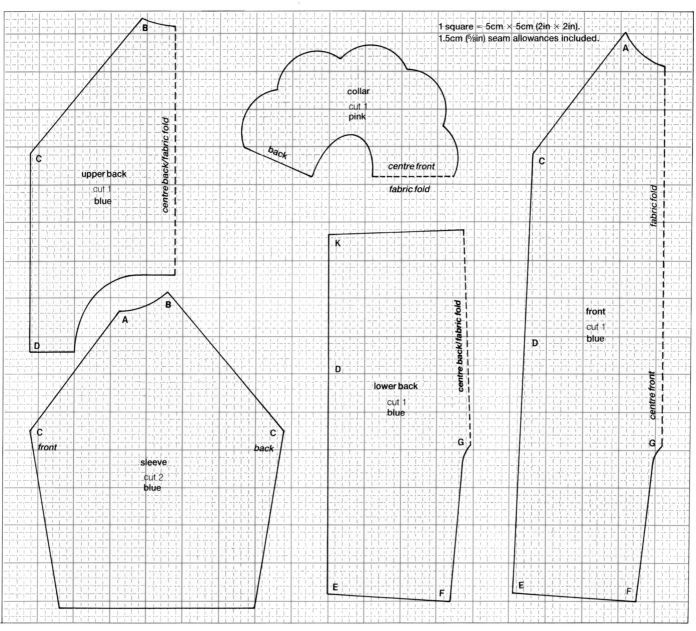

1 square = 5cm × 5cm (2in × 2in).
1.5cm (⁵⁄₈in) seam allowances included.

collar
cut 1
pink

back

centre front

fabric fold

upper back
cut 1
blue

centre back/fabric fold

front
cut 1
blue

fabric fold

centre front

lower back
cut 1
blue

centre back/fabric fold

front
back

sleeve
cut 2
blue

▦ Place collar to neck edge with right side of collar to wrong side of neck edge; pin and stitch. Neaten raw inside edge with bias binding. Turn collar to outside. Stitch on button and make worked loop at top of back neck opening.

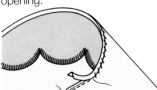

▦ Run a line of gathering stitches round each pompon circle. Pull up gathering stitches round a small amount of filling; fasten off. Stitch pompons in place on front of jump suit.

▦ Work a row of gathering stitches round ends of sleeves and legs.

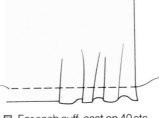

▦ For each cuff, cast on 40 sts. Work in K1, P1 rib for 5cm (2in).

Cast off. Stitch side seam of each cuff.

▦ For each ankle band, cast on 50 sts. Work in K1, P1 rib for 9cm (3½in). Cast off. Stitch side seam of each band.

▦ Place a knitted cuff to end of each sleeve; pin and stitch in place, pulling up gathering evenly to fit. Stitch ankle bands to base of each trouser leg in the same way.

33

ONE YEAR OLD ALREADY

A first birthday is a big moment and baby deserves a fancy outfit for the celebration. Boys can wear ribbons too, just like girls – stitched in a smart pattern to make one side of a reversible jacket. The ribbon fabric is made up first and then stitched to the floral lining with a light layer of wadding between for warmth.

Size: to fit a nine- to twelve-month-old baby.

MATERIALS

TROUSERS
50cm (⅝yd) of 114cm (45in) wide floral cotton furnishing fabric
70cm (¾yd) of 8cm (3¼in) wide ribbon
40cm (½yd) of 1.5cm (⅝in) wide elastic
Dressmakers' pattern paper
Matching thread

JACKET
60cm (¾yd) of 114cm (45in) wide floral furnishing fabric
60cm (¾yd) of 114cm (45in) wide curtain lining
60cm (¾yd) of 90cm (36in) wide wadding
1m (1yd) of 15cm (6in) wide ribbon
3m (3¼yd) of 4cm (1½in) wide ribbon
2m (2⅛yd) of 2.5cm (1in) wide ribbon
2m (2⅛yd) of 1.5cm (⅝in) wide ribbon
1.2m (1½yd) of 6mm (¼in) wide green ribbon
60cm (¾yd) of 6mm (¼in) wide pink ribbon
Dressmakers' pattern paper
Dressmakers' carbon paper
Matching thread

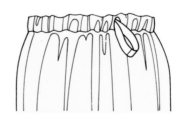

METHOD FOR TROUSERS

▦ Draw up pattern from diagram. Cut out following cutting instructions.
▦ Place a length of 8cm (3¼in) wide ribbon along base edge of each trouser leg, with right sides together; pin and stitch around base of trousers, continuing stitching around both sides of marked slit. Cut slit and snip corners. Fold the ribbon down.

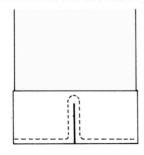

▦ Pin and stitch inner leg seams, with right sides together, continuing stitching through ribbon. Neaten and press open. Turn ribbon to the wrong side and handstitch in place.

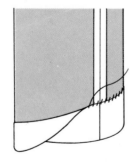

▦ With right sides together, pin and stitch trouser pieces together from centre front round to centre back. Snip curved seam.

▦ Turn under top edge for 2.5cm (1in), tuck under 6mm (¼in); pin and stitch in place, leaving an opening at one seam. Thread elastic through the waist casing; overlap ends for 1cm (⅜in) and stitch together. Push elastic into casing and stitch up opening.

METHOD FOR JACKET

▦ Draw up pattern from diagram.
▦ Mark the outline of the pattern on the curtain lining, using dressmakers' carbon paper. Place the ribbons, right side up, on the lining, completely covering the outlined jacket pattern; pin and topstitch ribbons in place.

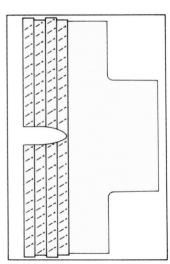

1 square = 5cm × 5cm (2in × 2in). 1.5cm (⅝in) seam allowances included.

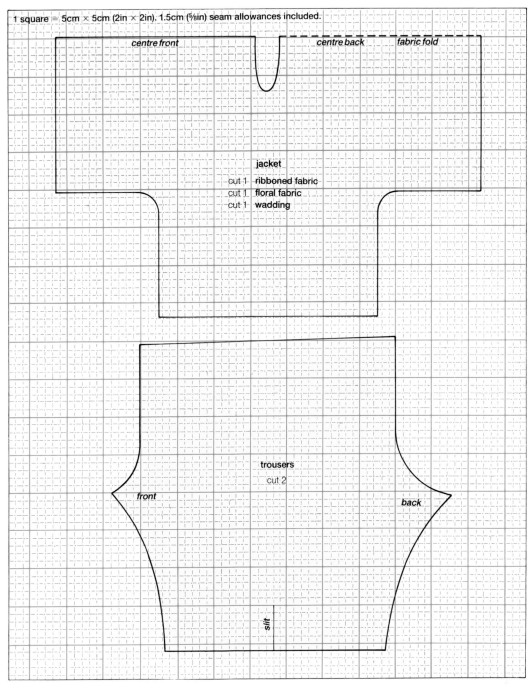

centre front   centre back   fabric fold

jacket
cut 1 ribboned fabric
cut 1 floral fabric
cut 1 wadding

trousers
cut 2

front   back

slit

■ Cut out one jacket in ribboned fabric, one in floral fabric and one in wadding. Tack the wadding to the wrong side of the floral print fabric. With right sides together, pin and stitch side/underarm seams on both jackets.
■ With right sides together, place the wadded jacket to ribbon jacket; pin and stitch front edges and around neck edge. Trim and turn to right side.
■ Turn in sleeve and jacket hems for 1.5cm (⅝in); pin and topstitch close to hem edge. Topstitch around neck edge and down front edges to match.

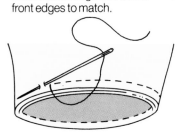

■ Topstitch vertically down the jacket at 4cm (1½in) intervals.
■ Cut 6mm (¼in) wide green ribbon into four equal pieces and cut 6mm (¼in) wide pink ribbon in half. Handstitch to jacket front, with top pair 4cm (1½in) down from neck edge and then at 10cm (4in) intervals, placing the pair of pink ribbons in the middle.

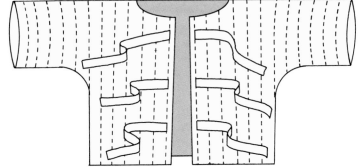

GOOD MORNING

If plain sewing gives you pleasure and time-consuming embroidery drives you to distraction, then these pink, painted cotton pyjamas are perfect for you. A simple stand collar and patch pockets are easy details to machine stitch, while the handwork is reduced to eight bold buttons for the front. Beautiful motifs, based on French wooden toys, are given for you to paint on; an instant, colourful effect.

Size: to fit a three-year-old.

MATERIALS

3m (3⅜yd) of 90cm (36in) wide pink cotton fabric	Eight 2cm (¾in) diameter buttons 60cm (24in) 2cm (¾in) elastic

METHOD

▣ Draw up patterns from diagram. Cut out following cutting instructions.

▣ To make up patch pockets, turn under top edge of each pocket for 6mm (¼in); pin and stitch. Turn a 2cm (¾in) wide facing to right side; pin and stitch sides. Snip corners. Turn facing to the wrong side of pocket; topstitch across top. Turn under seam allowance on side edges of pocket and place to front at marked positions; pin and topstitch pocket sides.

▣ Place front to back with right sides together; pin and stitch shoulder seams. Trim and neaten. Place sleeves to front/back with right sides together; pin and stitch. Trim and neaten. Press on to sleeve.

▣ Fold jacket with right sides together; pin and stitch side seams, continuing to stitch underarm seam to wrist. Trim and neaten.

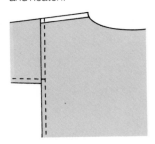

▣ Neaten edges of front facings. Fold facings to the right side for 6.5cm (2⅝in); pin and stitch top edges for 6.5cm (2⅝in). Fold facing to inside of jacket.

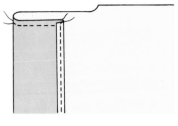

▣ Fold collar in half lengthways with right sides together; pin and stitch ends. Trim and turn to the right side. Place one long side of collar to right side of neck edge; pin and stitch. Trim and turn to inside. Turn under remaining edge of collar; pin and slipstitch in place.

▣ Mark and work four buttonholes down right-hand side of jacket. Stitch buttons to opposite side to match. Stitch buttons alongside buttonholes, to give a double-breasted effect.

▣ Turn up hem edge of jacket for 2cm (¾in), catching in base edges of pockets. Tuck under 6mm (¼in); pin and hem in place. Repeat for sleeve hems.

▣ With right sides together, stitch trouser centre front and back seams. Pin and stitch inner leg seams in a continuous line. Turn base of trouser legs up 6mm (¼in), then 2cm (¾in) to form hem. Stitch.

▣ Make waist casing as page 34.

HINTS FOR PAINTING MOTIFS

Before you start, mark the design on to the fabric using dressmakers' carbon paper: trace off the design, place the tracing on the fabric in the correct place, slide a sheet of carbon paper between the tracing and the fabric, shiny side down, and pin or hold firmly in place. Draw firmly over the lines of the design, then remove carbon and tracing. Pin the jacket on to a working board: over a layer of plastic and a layer of spare fabric. Try not to stretch the fabric as it will distort the motif.

▣ When working with fabric paints, use a soft dry brush, and rinse it well between each colour change. Paints can also be mixed together to provide extra colours. Before you begin, test the paint colours on a spare piece of fabric, as some paint colours can alter when applied to strong-coloured fabrics. Leave the fabric to dry, then fix the paint to the fabric by pressing with a very hot iron over a clean cotton cloth.

▣ Alternatively, use paint marker pens, which can produce very fine lines; however, they are not very good at filling in large areas of the same colour as it is inclined to go streaky. As these pens are indelible the paint does not have to be fixed on to the fabric, but be careful, as any mistakes cannot be removed.

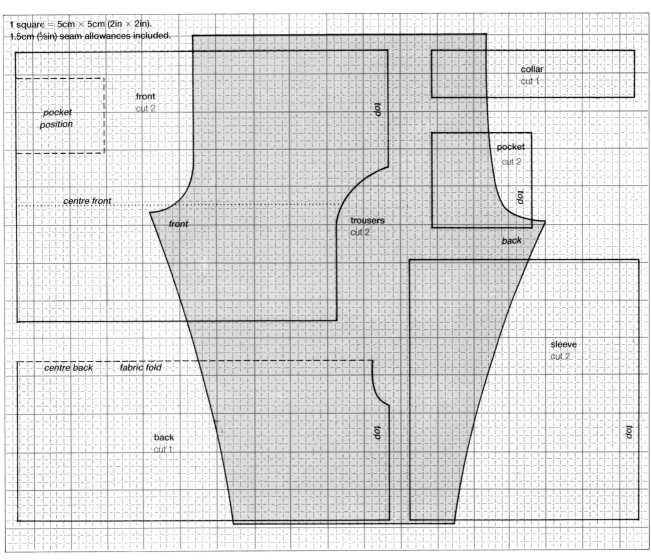

1 square = 5cm × 5cm (2in × 2in).
1.5cm (⅝in) seam allowances included.

pocket
position

front
cut 2

collar
cut 1

pocket
cut 2

top

top

centre front

front

trousers
cut 2

back

centre back   fabric fold

top

sleeve
cut 2

back
cut 1

top

Choose the motif designs for children's clothes from child-like objects and books. Enlist the child's help to pick the right one, as children have definite ideas about the clothes they want to wear. A good firm outline will be easy to fill in with paint on a fabric and bright colours will not only cheer up the garment but bring a touch of individuality and fun.

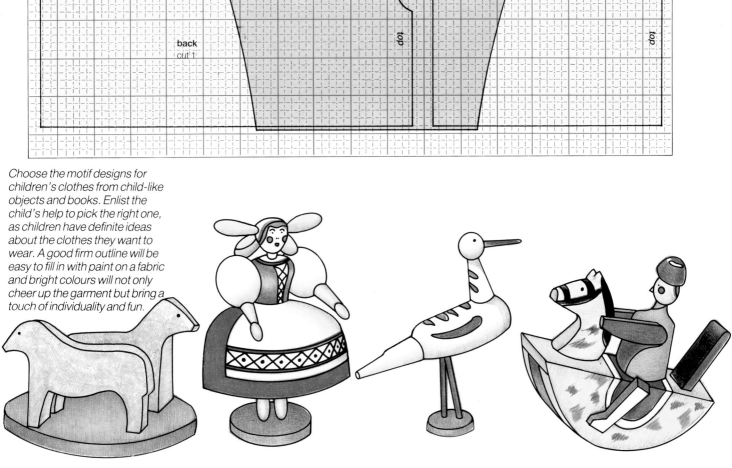

TUTTI FRUTTI

Delicious, delectable morsels – four pretty pinafores designed to melt the hardest heart. What better celebration of summer could there be? These fruity pinafores made of shiny chintz have straps criss-crossed at the back and stitched to a simple dirndl skirt. The padded shapes are quick to make, each one a perfect project for a holiday mood. Use the same idea for trousers for a jealous brother.

Size: to fit a four-year-old.

MATERIALS

70cm (¾yd) of 122cm (48in) wide glazed cotton for skirt and straps
Three 1cm (⅜in) diameter buttons
Oddments of fabric and wadding for fruit motifs and backing

Dressmakers' pattern paper
Embroidery cottons
Dressmakers' carbon paper
Matching thread

METHOD

To make basic skirt and straps.

▦ For the skirt cut one piece 122cm × 45cm (48in × 17¾in); a waistband 58cm × 9cm (23in × 3½in), and two straps each 122cm × 7cm (48in × 2¾in).

▦ Fold the skirt in half with right sides together. Pin and stitch, taking 1.5cm (⅝in) seam allowance, and leaving 15cm (6in) open at top. Turn in opening edges for 1.5cm (⅝in); pin.

▦ Work two rows of gathering stitches round top of skirt, 1.5cm (⅝in) from top raw edge. Pull up gathers evenly to 52cm (20⅝in) and stitch over the gathers to hold in place.

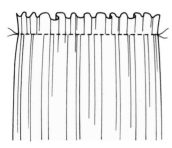

▦ Place waistband on skirt with right sides together, extending the band for 4.5cm (1¾in) at one side and 1.5cm (⅝in) at the other; and stitch. Fold band in half lengthways with right sides together; pin and stitch ends and

along extensions. Refold with wrong sides together, turn under remaining raw edge and slipstitch over previous stitches.

▦ Work a buttonhole on the right back waistband at centre back and one on the right and left waistband, 6cm(2½in) from centre back. Stitch the button to centre back on the left waistband.

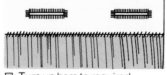

▦ Turn up hem to required length, then tuck under 6mm (¼in); pin and hem in place.

▦ Fold each strap in half lengthways with right sides together; pin and stitch the long side. Refold with seam to centre; stitch one short end. Turn.

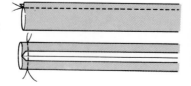

METHOD FOR WATER MELON

▦ Draw up motif to size and mark the outline of the shape on a piece of white fabric, using dressmakers' carbon paper. Cut out, adding a 3cm (1¼in) margin all round.

▦ Using this as a pattern, cut out one shape from the wadding and one from pink fabric for backing.

▦ Place the white and pink fabrics with wrong sides together, sandwiching the wadding in between; tack.

▦ Mark and cut out the 'skin'

from green fabric. Tack in place over marked outline. Mark and cut out pink 'flesh' and tack over outline.

▦ Zigzag stitch all round 'skin' and then 'flesh' with matching thread. Embroider 'pips' in dark brown embroidery cotton in satin stitch. Trim away excess fabric from around the motif.

METHOD FOR STRAWBERRY

▦ Draw up motif to size and mark and cut out the shape, as above, from two layers of pink

fabric and one layer of wadding, adding a 3cm (1¼in) margin all round.

▦ Place the fabrics with wrong sides together, sandwiching the wadding in between; tack. Zigzag stitch all round with matching pink thread.

▦ Mark and cut out leaf shape from green fabric. Place over strawberry, tack; then zigzag stitch in place, using matching green thread.

▦ Embroider French knots all over strawberry in yellow embroidery cotton. Trim away excess fabric around the motif.

METHOD FOR BANANA

▦ Draw up motif to size and mark and cut out the shape, as above, from two layers of yellow fabric and one layer of wadding, adding a 3cm (1¼in) margin all round.

▦ Place the fabrics with wrong sides together, sandwiching the wadding in between; tack.

▦ Zigzag stitch all round the outer edge and round the outline of each banana, using brown thread.

▦ Work the ridges in running stitch and the banana edges in

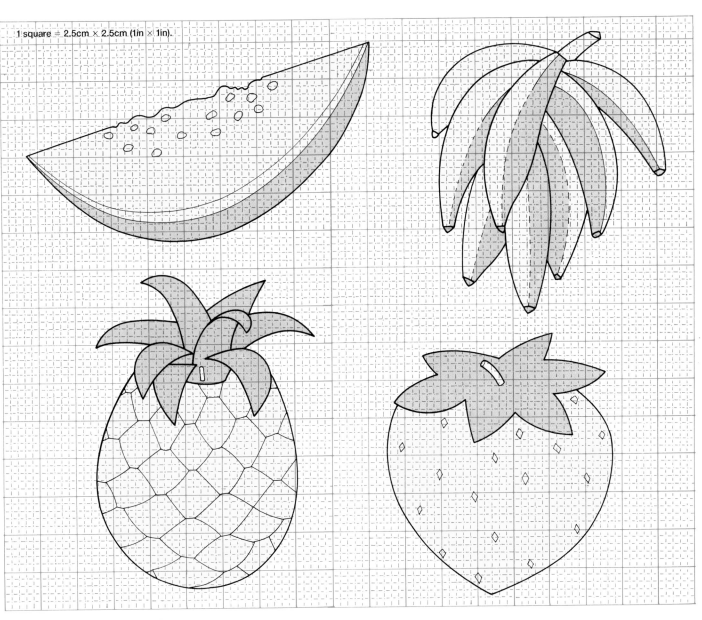

1 square = 2.5cm × 2.5cm (1in × 1in).

stem stitch, using brown embroidery cotton. Trim away excess fabric from around the motif.

METHOD FOR PINEAPPLE

▦ Draw up motif to size and mark and cut out the shape, as above, from two layers of yellow fabric and one layer of wadding, adding a 3cm (1¼in) margin all round.
▦ Place the fabrics with wrong sides together, sandwiching the wadding in between; tack.
▦ Stitch round the outline of the

fruit using green and zigzag round the outer edge in yellow.
▦ Mark and cut out the leaf from green fabric; tack to top of fruit.
▦ Zigzag stitch all round leaf using matching thread. Trim away excess fabric from around the motif.

TO COMPLETE PINAFORE

▦ For the strawberry, bananas and pineapple, centre the motif on the front of the skirt; pin and handstitch in place at the back with invisible stitches.
▦ Place closed ends of straps

behind the top of the fruit and stitch in place.
▦ Take the straps over the shoulders to cross over at the back. Mark positions of buttonholes.
▦ Trim off straps to required length, turn in raw edges and slipstitch. Stitch on buttons at marked positions.
▦ For water melon, pin and stitch straps to the front of the skirt behind the waistband, 5cm (2in) on either side of centre front.
▦ Take straps over the shoulders and complete as before.

▦ Pin and handstitch water melon to straps at the front.

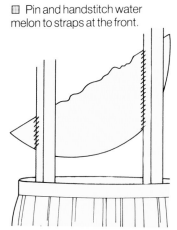

SMART STEPHANIE

Classic pleats like these have an ageless charm and suit all types, all ages. The dress is made of rectangles of fabric, pleated and tacked in place before it is sewn together.

Size to fit any size.

MATERIALS

To calculate the amount of material required, measure each section as described and allow for the length by three times the width measurement.

This will allow for the pleating.
One 1.5cm (⅝in) button
Matching thread
1.3cm (½in) wide bias binding

METHOD

Take the following measurements:
A – chest
B – neckline depth
C – length of dress
D – shoulder width
E – armhole length
F – measurement around shoulders
When cutting out, add hem allowances and 1.5cm (⅝in) seam allowances.

▦ The main part of the dress is an oblong folded up into 3cm (1¼in) knife pleats; the width after pleating should be the same size as the chest A plus 4cm (1½in); the length should equal C.

▦ The straps that link the back to the front are two pleated oblongs: they measure, after pleating, the width of D by twice the length B.

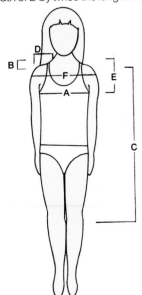

▦ The sleeve frills are two pleated oblongs 8cm (3¾in) wide by twice the length E.

▦ Mark the centre front of the main oblong. To make the armholes, cut rectangles out of the main part of the body parallel to the centre front: the depth of

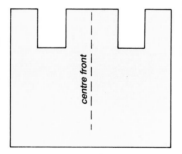

the armhole equals E minus B. For the width, take A away from F and divide the remainder by 2.

▦ Pin and tack all pleats. Stitch across pleats to hold them: at armhole level; 4cm (1½in) from neckline; and a row in between.

▦ To make up the dress, first pin and stitch the centre back seam to within 15cm (6in) of the neck edge, taking a 1.5cm (⅝in) seam allowance. Fold and stitch hems to wrong side along back opening. Neaten neckline edge with bias binding.

▦ Work a button loop at back neck edge and add a button.

▦ Pin and stitch the straps in place, completing armholes. Neaten lower edges of armholes with bias binding. Pin and stitch sleeve frills in place.

▦ Turn up the lower edge of dress and sleeve frills to the required length; pin and hem.

SHIPMATES

A smart sailor frock to see a girl through all childhood's adventures, even if they are only voyages in the unknown world of the imagination . . . Make them in wool, with mother-of-pearl buttons and satin or grosgrain ribbon, like they did in Edwardian days. The skirt is simply gathered on to a loose-fitting top that leaves enough room for a blouse, T-shirt or vest underneath for winter warmth.

Size: to fit an eight- to ten-year-old.

MATERIALS

1.9m (2⅛yd) of 140/150cm (54/56in) wide wool mixture
5.5m (6yd) of 1cm (⅜in) wide white braid
60cm (¾yd) of 2.5cm (1in) wide white ribbon

Four 1cm (⅜in) mother-of-pearl buttons
Press fastener
Dressmakers' pattern paper
Matching thread

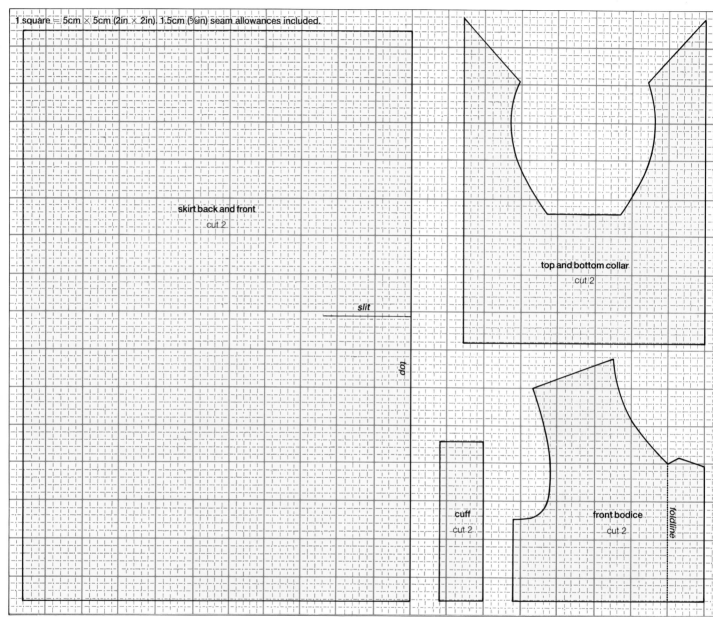

1 square = 5cm × 5cm (2in × 2in). 1.5cm (⅝in) seam allowances included.

skirt back and front
cut 2

slit

top

top and bottom collar
cut 2

cuff
cut 2

front bodice
cut 2

foldline

METHOD

▦ Draw up patterns from diagrams. Cut out following cutting instructions.

▦ To make an opening, cut a 10cm (4in) long slit in the centre front of the skirt, as marked on the pattern. Cut a straight strip of fabric 20cm × 4.5cm (8in × 1¾in). Pin strip down one side of slit and then up the second side, keeping right sides together; stitch close to edge. Fold the strip through centre to wrong side. Turn under raw edge for 3mm (⅛in);

and slipstitch over previous stitching. Press to wrong side.

▦ Place skirt pieces with right sides together; pin and stitch side seams. Work two rows of gathering stitches 1.5cm (⅝in) from top of skirt. Pull up gathers evenly until skirt top measures 80cm (31½in); stitch over gathers to

hold in place.

▦ Place front bodice pieces to back bodice with right sides together; pin and stitch side and shoulder seams.

▦ Place skirt to bodice with right sides together, matching side seams and matching fold line of front bodice to edge of concealed front opening; pin and stitch. Neaten front edges of bodice; then fold front bodice edges to wrong side. Topstitch front opening close to edge from top to base.

▦ Fold sleeves with right sides

together; pin and stitch underarm seams. Work two rows of gathering stitches around top of each sleeve between A and B

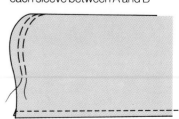

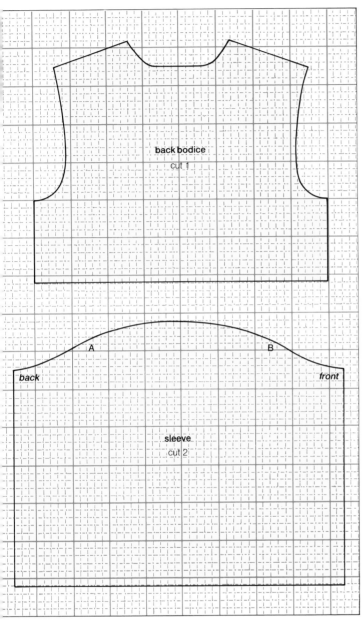

◫ Place sleeves in armholes with right sides together, matching underarm seams and pulling up gathers evenly to fit; pin and stitch in place.

◫ Work two rows of gathering stitches around base of each sleeve. Pull up gathers evenly until base measures 18cm (7in); stitch over gathers to hold in place.

◫ Stitch each cuff into a ring. Fold in half lengthways, wrong sides together.

◫ Pin and stitch one edge of cuff to edge of sleeve. Turn under remaining edge and slipstitch to wrong side over previous stitches.

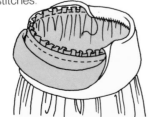

◫ Place collars with right sides together; pin and stitch leaving neck edges open. Trim and turn collar to the right side. Place bottom layer of collar to neck edge with right sides together; pin and stitch. Turn under raw edge of top collar and slipstitch over previous stitches.

◫ Turn skirt up to the required length, then tuck under 6mm (¼in) and hem in place.

◫ Pin and topstitch two rows of braid around base edge of skirt, 6mm (¼in) from bottom edge and 6mm (¼in) apart. Pin and topstitch two rows of braid around the collar and one row around each cuff in the same way.

◫ Work two horizontal buttonholes centrally in front opening, stitching buttons to the opposite side to match. Stitch a press fastener to bodice at collar position. Tie the ribbon into a large bow and sew to dress over press fastener.

LIKE A FEATHER IN THE WIND

These little creatures float in a pastel haze of organdie. Cut to a basic apron pattern with cross ties at the back, they have their variations, like themes in music: the yellow one has tiny pintucks on the bodice and a hem in points; deeper tucks are grouped in threes on the blue; the green one has fine tucks on frills and hem; there are scalloped edges on the red; and the pink has spaced tucks and petal hems. Add a simple pair of plain pantaloons and you have perfection plus!

Size: to fit a five- to six-year-old.

MATERIALS

DRESS	PANTALOONS
2m (2⅛yd) of 112cm (44in) wide organdie	1m (1yd) of 90cm (36in) wide cotton poplin
One 2cm (¾in) diameter button	60cm (¾yd) of elastic
Dressmakers' pattern paper	Dressmakers' pattern paper
Matching thread	Matching thread

METHOD FOR DRESSES

▣ Draw up patterns from diagrams. Cut out following cutting instructions.

▣ Follow the diagrams for the tucked areas on the chosen pinafore; the sections marked **e** are the areas to be reproduced at the base of the skirt. Fold up wide tucks or pintucks on skirt and frills: stitch and then press downwards.

▣ If the chosen pinafore has scalloped hem and frill edges, trace off the scalloped edge from the diagram and mark on the fabric 1cm (⅜in) away from the edge. Work round the marked lines with a tight zigzag stitch (on a machine) or buttonhole stitch (by hand); trim away excess fabric.

▣ For the pinafore with double frills, make two pairs of frills, one 8cm (3¼in) wide and the other 5cm (2in) wide; work scalloped edges as above.

▣ If the chosen pinafore has plain hem and frill edges, turn double 1.5cm (⅝in) hems; pin and stitch.

▣ Measure up 40cm (16in) from hemmed edge of skirt and cut off excess fabric around skirt top.

▣ Turn a double 1.5cm (⅝in) hem

along the side edges of the skirt; pin and stitch.

▣ Fold the bib tucks, following diagram for chosen pinafore and leaving 1.5cm (⅝in) at the neck edge; pin and stitch wide tucks or pintucks.

▣ Work two rows of gathering stitches round the base of each frill and pull up until frill measures 50cm (20in); stitch over gathers to hold. Trim bib at base until bib front measures 18cm (7in) from neck edge.

▣ With right sides together, place frills to bib; pin and tack.

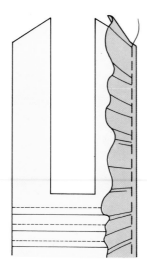

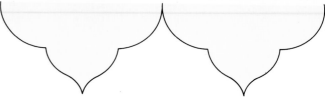

■ Place bib lining to bib with right sides together; pin and stitch neck and outer edges of bib straps catching in frills and leaving lower edge open. Trim and turn to right side.

■ Work a row of gathering stitches round the top edge of skirt and pull up to 60cm (24in); stitch over gathers to hold. With right sides together, place one waistband to skirt; pin and stitch. Fold up waistband to right side.

■ With right sides together, place bib bottom centrally to upper edge of waistband; pin and tack.

■ With right sides together, place other waistband to first waistband, sandwiching bib in between; pin and stitch upper edge through all layers. Turn to wrong side, tuck in raw edge and slipstitch to skirt.

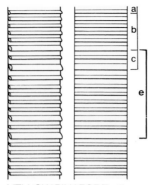

YELLOW PINAFORE **a** 3mm (⅛in); **b** five pintucks with 5mm (¼in) spaces; **c** one 5mm (¼in) tuck, one pintuck, one 5mm (¼in) tuck.

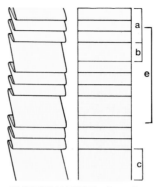

BLUE PINAFORE **a** three 1cm (⅜in) tucks; **b** 2cm (¾in) spaces; **c** 3cm (1¼in)

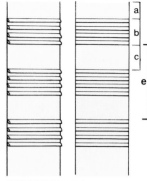

GREEN PINAFORE **a** 1.5cm (⅝in); **b** four pintucks with 5mm (¼in) spaces; **c** 2.5cm (1in) space

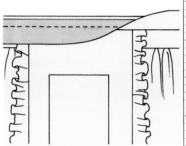

■ Fold apron strings in half lengthways; pin and stitch raw edges, leaving one end open. Trim and turn to right side.

■ Make two small pleats at raw end until string measures 4cm (1½in); push ends inside waistband ends; pin and stitch to close, catching in string.

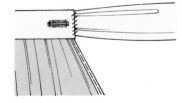

■ Work a buttonhole at the end of each bib strap and one on the right side of the waistband. Stitch a button to the end of the left side of the waistband to match.

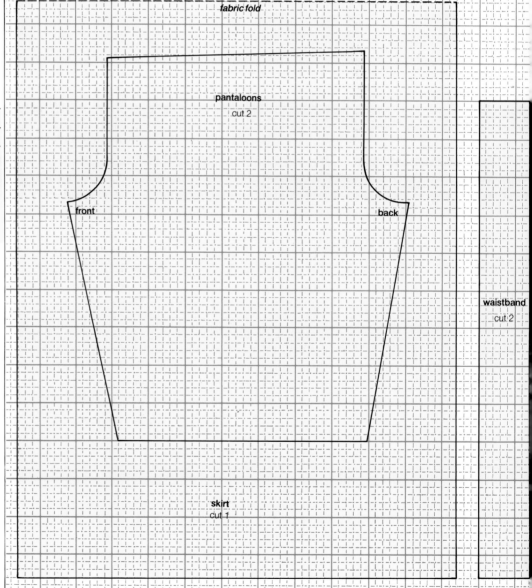

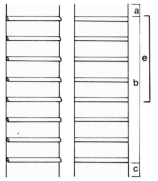 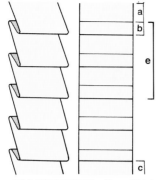

All the pintucks are 2mm (⅛in) wide. After stitching the pintucks press them downwards.

The area marked ***e*** *on each diagram is the tucked area to be reproduced at the base of the skirt.*

RED PINAFORE ***a*** *1.2cm (½in);* ***b*** *eight pintucks with 2cm (¾in) spaces;* ***c*** *1.3cm (½in)*

PINK PINAFORE ***a*** *2cm (¾in) space;* ***b*** *1cm (⅜in) tuck;* ***c*** *1cm (⅜in) space*

1 square = 5cm × 5cm (2in × 2in). 1.5cm (⅝in) seam allowances included.

apron strings
cut 2

fold

bib
cut 1

bib lining
cut 1

frill
cut 2

fold

METHOD FOR PANTALOONS

▦ Draw up patterns from diagram. Cut out following cutting instructions.

▦ Place trousers with right sides together; pin and stitch centre and inner leg seams.

▦ Turn up a 2.5cm (1in) hem at the base of each leg, then tuck under 6mm (¼in); pin and hem in place.

▦ Turn down 2cm (¾in) at waist edge, then tuck under 6mm (¼in); pin and stitch close to edge, leaving an opening at one seam. Thread elastic through waist casing; overlap ends for 1cm (⅜in) and stitch together. Push elastic into casing and stitch up opening.

GALA TEA

Take a little extra loving care to produce a dress for a grand occasion. Classic fabrics such as crisp white cotton piqué invite the extra stitchery, lace appliqué, braid and ribbons that make a dress unique, nostalgic. This sleeveless masterpiece with an over-bodice flatters a girl's best features and ignores her lack of waist with tact. No one is above that kind of flattery.

Size: to fit a four-year-old.

MATERIALS

1.6m (1¾yd) of 114cm (45in) wide fine white piqué	40cm (½yd) of 6mm (¼in) wide lace (F)
5m (5½yd) of scalloped braid (A)	25cm (10in) of 1.5cm (⅝in) wide braid (G)
2m (2⅛yd) of 2.5cm (1in) wide fancy ribbon (B)	10cm (4in) of flowery braid (I)
7m (7¾yd) of 6mm (¼in) wide lace (C)	Four 1.3cm (½in) diameter buttons
1m (1yd) of 1cm (⅜in) wide open-work insertion (D)	Dressmakers' pattern paper
40cm (½yd) of binding with picots (E)	Matching thread

METHOD

▦ Draw up patterns from diagrams. Cut out following cutting instructions.

▦ Following guidelines on the diagram, place lengths of ribbon (B) on the front and back bodice, pin and stitch down the lengths. Tack lace (C) parallel to the edge of ribbons (B); pin and stitch.

▦ With right sides together, pin and stitch shoulder seams. Repeat for yoke lining. With right sides together, place the scalloped braid (A) with straight edge along the base and armhole edges of the bodice; pin and stitch. Fold scalloped edge of braid to right side of base and armhole edges, folding the raw fabric edge under to the wrong side of garment.

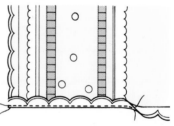

▦ Place bodice and bodice lining with right sides together; pin and stitch centre back edges together. Turn to right side. Turn in seam allowance along neck edge of both bodice and bodice lining.

▦ Position braid (G) on edge of left back bodice; pin and stitch. Place binding (E) between neck edges of bodice and lining; pin and tack neck edges together. Position lace (F) round the neck edge of bodice; pin and stitch in place through all layers.

▦ Turn in lining edges and handstitch bodice and bodice lining together at armhole and lower edges.

bottom to slip in the skirt.

▦ Topstitch the four lines across the front (see photograph/pattern). Cut out flowers from flowery braid (I) and stitch by hand to bodice at each intersection.

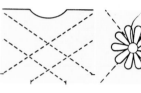

▦ Turn under narrow hems on each side of front skirt; pin and tack. Make a 4.5cm (1¾in) wide horizontal tuck round the base of the skirt, 13cm (5in) up from base edge; stitch. Position a length of ribbon (B) along each side edge of front skirt; pin and topstitch.

▦ Turn under narrow hems on sides and base of back skirt; pin and tack. Make a tuck round the back panel in the same way as for the front.

▦ Place back to back panel with right sides together, inserting open-work intersection (D); pin and stitch. Position lace (C) on either side of intersection; pin and stitch.

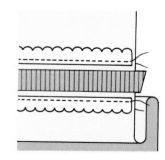

▦ To join back skirt to front, place the free edge of ribbon (B) over side of skirt; pin and topstitch. Position lace (C) along edges of ribbon (B); pin and stitch.

▣ To make an opening in skirt, cut a 13cm (5in) long slit in the centre back of skirt, as marked on the pattern. Cut a straight strip of fabric 26cm × 3.5cm (10¼in × 1⅜in). Pin strip down one side of slit and then up the second side, keeping right sides together; stitch close to edge. Fold the strip through centre to wrong side. Turn under raw edge for 3mm (⅛in), and slipstitch over previous stitching.

▣ Work two rows of gathering stitches round top edge of skirt front and back omitting ribbons (B). Draw up gathers so front skirt measures same as lower edge of front bodice with ribbons (B) matching. Draw up back gathers so skirt is 5cm(2in) wider at each side than lower edge of back bodice with centre openings matching.

▣ Lay bodice over skirt so bodice overlaps by 4.5cm(1¾in). Topstitch together with a zigzag stitch, continuing stitching over the 5cm(2in) of skirt between front and back bodice to hold gathers in position.

▣ Place scalloped braid (A) around right side of one waistband; pin and tack. Place second waistband to first with right sides together; pin and stitch all round, catching in braid and leaving an opening for turning. Trim and turn to right side; stitch up opening.

▣ Position waistband 4.5cm(1¾in) above lower edge of bodice. Pin and stitch in place along lower edge of waistband starting at armhole edge of bodice back.

▣ Work three vertical buttonholes on the left-hand opening on the braid and a loop at neck edge. Stitch buttons to the opposite side to match.

▣ Turn up hem to the required length, then tuck under 6mm (¼in) and hem in place.

Position the ribbons and braids to the front, back and waistband in the same order, working in neat rows, giving the armholes and waistband a patterned edge. The effect is stunning and will bring that certain 'something' to a plain white dress. Little girls love to have just one special dress in their wardrobes and this is it!

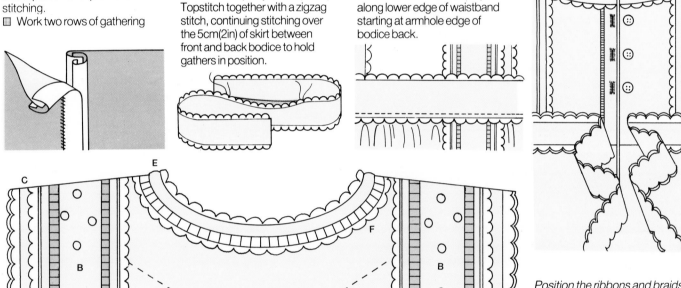

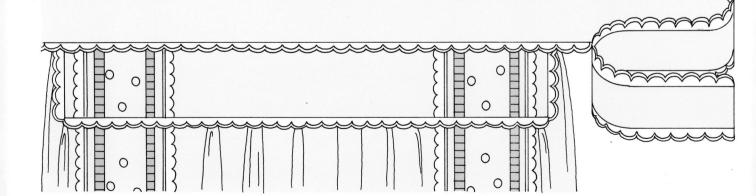

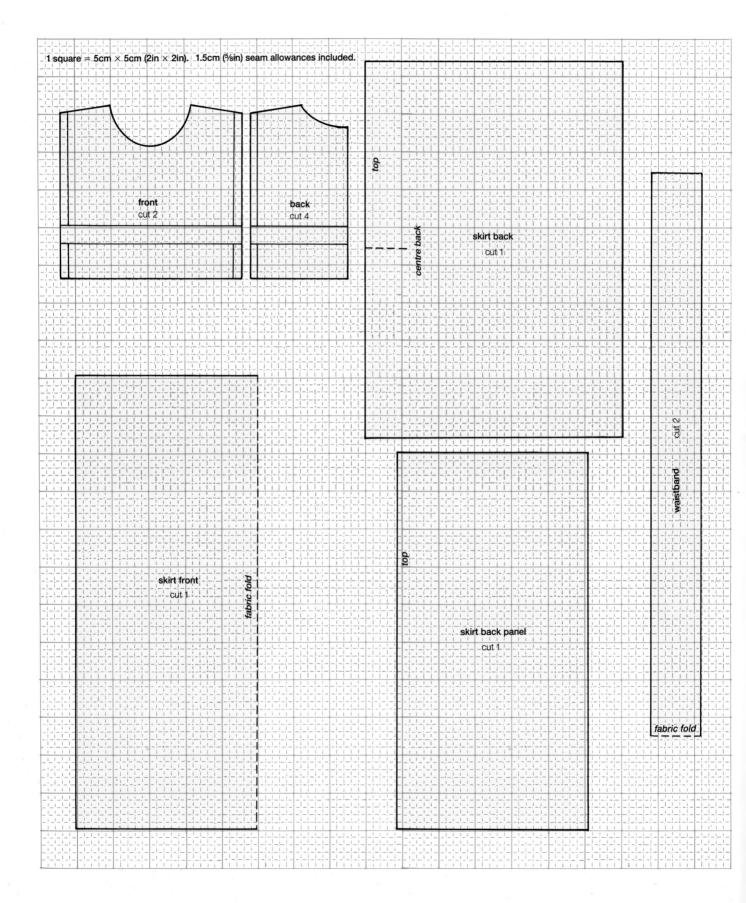

1 square = 5cm × 5cm (2in × 2in). 1.5cm (⅝in) seam allowances included.

front
cut 2

back
cut 4

top

centre back

skirt back
cut 1

waistband

cut 2

skirt front
cut 1

fabric fold

top

skirt back panel
cut 1

fabric fold

FULL SPEED AHEAD

A young boy's best blouson jacket for practicality and dash. Smart grey flannel keeps him warm and the generous raglan sleeves are comfortable, too. The ribbing for collar, cuffs and waistband is quick to knit and easy to stitch on. And what could be a simpler decoration than touch-and-close stripes and shapes in all colours, for the sportsman on the move? It's easy for him to open and close this jacket – after all, doesn't he like his independence at an early age?

Size: to fit a four-year-old.

MATERIALS

90cm (1yd) of 150cm (60in) wide grey flannel

2 cm (¾in) wide touch-and-close fastening: 55cm (22in) of yellow; 65cm (25½in) of red; 75cm (30in) of blue and 25cm (10in) of green

One 50g (2oz) ball of Pingouin Fine + in blue, red, yellow and green

One pair of 4mm (size 8) knitting needles

Dressmakers' pattern paper

Matching thread

METHOD

▣ Draw up patterns from diagrams. Cut out following cutting instructions.

▣ With right sides together, pin and stitch sleeves along upper arm seam AB. Pink the raw edges and press seams open. Topstitch 6mm (¼in) on either side of seams. Using the soft half of the touch-and-close fastening, place one length of blue 8cm (3¼in) above line CD. Above it, add a length of red and then yellow, spacing each length 2cm (¾in) apart; pin and topstitch in place, using matching thread.

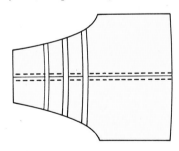

▣ With right sides together, pin and stitch sleeve to armhole edges. Pink the raw edges, press seams open and topstitch 6mm (¼in) on either side of seams.

▣ Fold jacket with right sides together; pin and stitch side seams from waist to wrist on each side. Pink the raw edges, press seams open and topstitch 6mm (¼in) on either side of seams.

▣ To neaten front edges, turn in front facing on each side of jacket along marked line; pin and tack.

▣ For lower border, cast on 136 sts in blue yarn. Work six rows of P2, K2 rib, then six rows in red, six rows in yellow and two rows in

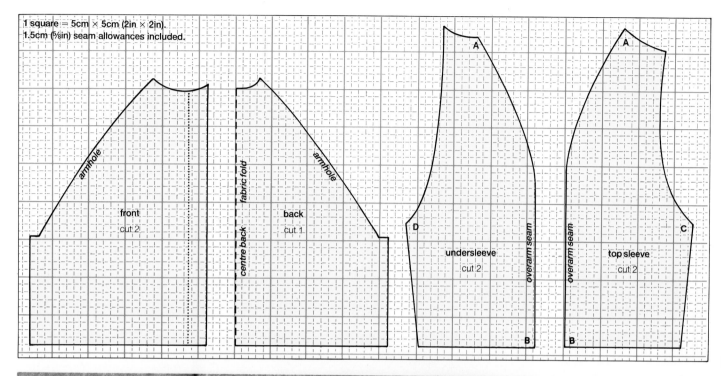

1 square = 5cm × 5cm (2in × 2in).
1.5cm (⅝in) seam allowances included.

armhole

front
cut 2

centre back · fabric fold

back
cut 1

armhole

A

D

undersleeve
cut 2

overarm seam

B

A

overarm seam

top sleeve
cut 2

C

B

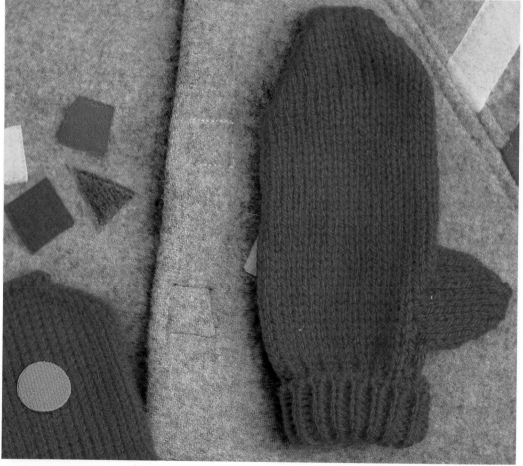

green. cast off.

▥ For collar neckband, cast on
70 sts in blue yarn. Work two
rows of P2, K2 rib, then two rows
in red and two rows in yellow.
Cast off.

▥ For each wristband, cast on
40 sts in blue yarn. Work six rows
of P2, K2 rib, six rows in red and
six rows in yellow. Cast off.

▥ Stitch the wristbands to form
rings, then stitch one to lower
edge of each sleeve, slightly
gathering up sleeve edge evenly
to fit. Stitch knitted lower band to
lower edge of jacket, gathering
up jacket edge evenly to fit. Stitch
the knitted neckband in place.

▥ Cut seven small squares of
touch-and-close fastening from
the different colours. Stitch one
half of each piece to right side of
right front and the opposite half to
underside of left front. Stitch
small pieces of fastening to
decorate back and fronts.

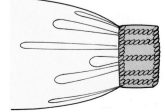

PLASTIC PRACTICALITY

Small boys love splashing through rain and puddles and they'll be well protected in this bold bright pvc raincoat. You'll need a sharp needle for stitching the pvc, and be sure to use tissue paper or a roller foot to help the fabric go under the presser foot. Your efforts are rewarded: there's no need to neaten the edges and eyelets and the stud fasteners snap on in seconds.

Size: to fit an eighteen-month- to two-year-old.

MATERIALS

1m (1yd) of 120cm (48in) wide
    patterned pvc
Two 5mm (¼in) diameter eyelets
Four press stud fasteners

70cm (¾yd) of narrow cord
Adhesive tape
Dressmakers' pattern paper
Matching thread

METHOD

▦ Draw up patterns from diagrams. Cut out following cutting instructions.
▦ Turn down the right side of each pocket top for 2cm (¾in); hold with tape and stitch in place at sides. Snip corners and turn facing to inside pocket. Stitch.
▦ Turn under seam allowance on all remaining edges; hold with tape.
▦ Place pockets on fronts at marked positions; hold with tape and topstitch in place close to outer edges, removing tape as you work.

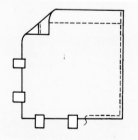

▦ Place sleeves to fronts with right sides together; hold with tape and stitch in place. Repeat, to stitch back to sleeves. Trim down seam allowance.
▦ Fold, so that back and fronts have right sides together; hold with tape and stitch side seams, continuing along underarm sleeve seams. Trim down seam allowance.

▦ Place hood pieces with right sides together; hold with tape and stitch curved seam. Trim down seam allowance.
▦ Fix an eyelet into hood on each side at marked positions, following manufacturer's instructions. Turn under front edge of hood along marked line, hold with tape and topstitch hem in place.
▦ Place hood to neck edge, with right sides together and front edges of hood to centre front; hold with tape and stitch in place. Trim seam allowance.
▦ Turn under a 2.5cm (1in) hem at the base of each sleeve; hold with tape; and topstitch in place. Stitch a similar hem along base edge of coat.
▦ Turn in facing along marked line; topstitch in place. Turn under neck and hem edge and handstitch.
▦ Fix press stud fasteners in place at marked positions, following manufacturer's instructions.
▦ Thread cord through eyelets in hood and knot both ends.

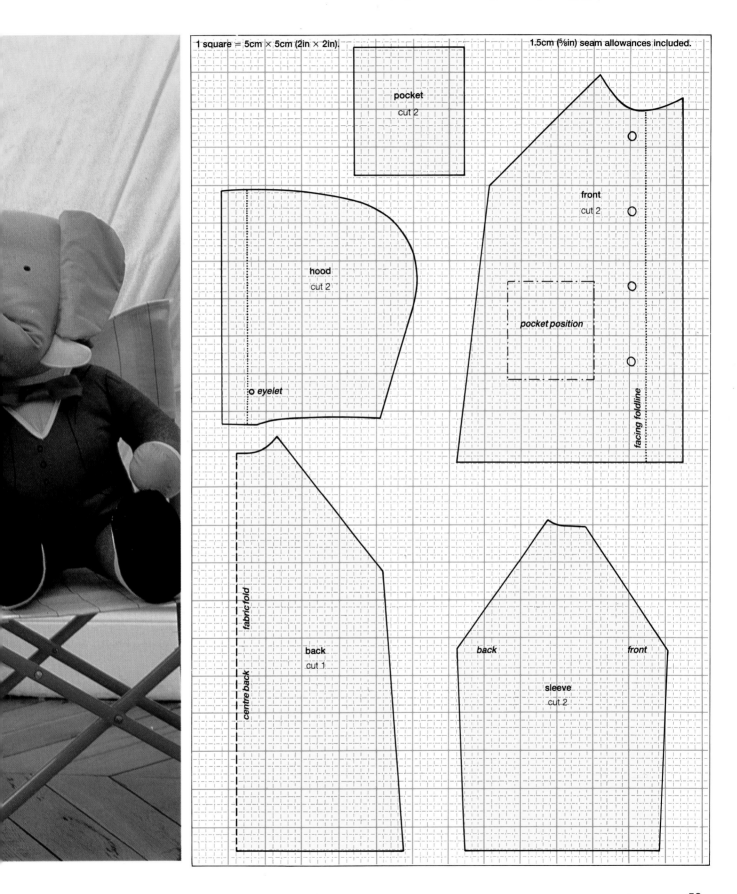

1 square = 5cm × 5cm (2in × 2in).

1.5cm (⅝in) seam allowances included.

pocket
cut 2

hood
cut 2

o *eyelet*

front
cut 2

pocket position

facing foldline

fabric fold

centre back

back
cut 1

back

front

sleeve
cut 2

PATCHWORK PARKAS

With large lined hoods and pockets big enough for children's special objects, these canvas parkas are the perfect solution to the cold outdoors. Make them in a combination of bright or earthy colours – with such practical garments, who says winter exercise needs to be a chore? Patterns are given for parkas to fit a four-year-old and a twelve-year-old, but they are cut big enough to last youngsters a good few years.

Size: to fit a four-year-old or twelve-year-old.

MATERIALS

150cm (60in) wide canvas – work out how much you need in each colour by drawing up the patterns and then making a cutting plan
2m (2⅛yd) of cord (four-year-old) or
2.5m (2¾yd) of cord (twelve-year-old)
Nine press stud fasteners

Four 8mm (⅜in) diameter eyelets
1.5m (1⅝yd) of 2.5cm (1in) wide bias binding (four-year-old) or
1.7m (1⅞yd) of 2.5cm (1in) wide bias binding (twelve-year-old)
1.3cm (½in) wide bias binding, for binding pockets
Dressmakers' pattern paper
Matching thread

METHOD

▦ Draw up patterns from diagram. Cut out from the desired colours.

▦ Join all the sections together with flat fell seams, unless otherwise stated.

▦ Place upper backs with right sides together; pin and stitch centre back seam.

▦ Pin upper back to lower back and stitch. Pin upper fronts to lower fronts and stitch.

▦ Fold welt in half lengthways with right sides together; pin and stitch sides with plain seams. Trim and turn to right side.

▦ Pin and tack welt to front, along marked lower pocket line, with right sides together and raw edges to centre line. Place first pocket lining right side down over welt, pin and stitch through all layers on lower marked line.

▦ Place second pocket lining right side down in position along top marked line, overlapping lower stitching line by 6mm (¼in); pin and stitch in place along top marked line.

▦ Cut along pocket centre line to within 6mm (¼in) of ends, then cut into each corner. Turn pocket linings through opening to wrong side and press; pin and stitch linings together, leaving edges at centre front of jacket free (these will be stitched with the jacket).

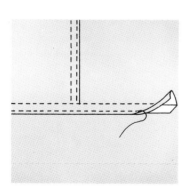

▦ Mark each pocket position with rows of tacking stitches: one row around the pocket position and one across the centre.

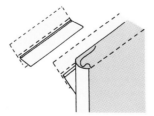

Large Parka (yellow pattern pieces)

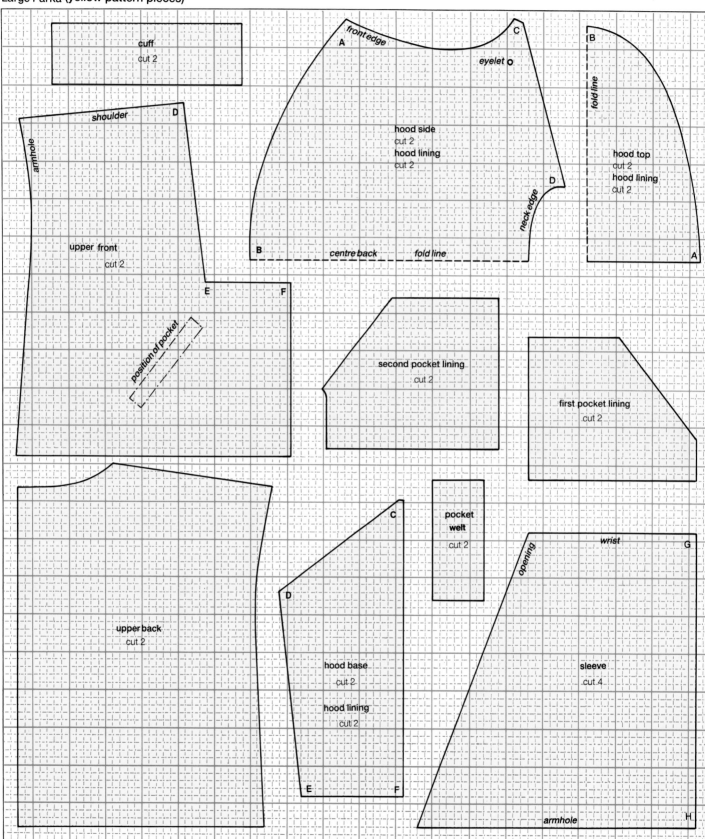

cuff
cut 2

front edge

A

C

eyelet ○

B

fold line

hood side
cut 2
hood lining
cut 2

hood top
cut 2
hood lining
cut 2

shoulder   D

armhole

D

neck edge

upper front
cut 2

B   centre back   fold line   A

E   F

position of pocket

second pocket lining
cut 2

first pocket lining
cut 2

C

pocket
welt
cut 2

opening   wrist   G

D

upper back
cut 2

hood base
cut 2

hood lining
cut 2

sleeve
cut 4

E   F

armhole   H

1 square = 5cm × 5cm (2in × 2in). 1.5cm (⅝in) seam allowances included.

F front facing cut 2 E

E F

front facing cut 2

first pocket lining cut 2

pocket welt cut 2

shoulder
armhole
D
upper front cut 2
E F
position of pocket

second pocket lining cut 2

C
D
hood base cut 2
hood lining cut 2
E F

upper back cut 2

B
fold line
hood top cut 2
hood lining cut 2
A

lower back cut 1
lower front cut 2
fabric fold
centre front
centre back

lower front cut 2
fabric fold
centre front
lower back cut 1
centre back

A front edge C eyelet o
hood side cut 2
hood lining cut 2
D
B centre back fold line
neck edge

wrist G
opening
sleeve cut 4
D
armhole H

cuff cut 2

▦ Fold bias binding evenly in half over raw edges of pocket lining, omitting centre front edges; pin and stitch.

▦ On right side, fold up welt; pin and topstitch to jacket at both ends. Repeat to make up second pocket in the same way.

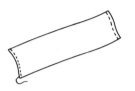

▦ Place fronts to back; pin and stitch shoulder seams. Stitch both sleeves from G to H. Place sleeves to front/back with right sides together; pin and stitch. Fold front to back with right sides together; pin and stitch plain side seams, continuing stitching along underarm seam of sleeve, ending 8cm (3¼in) from wrist to allow for wrist opening.

▦ Turn under a narrow double hem along either side of each sleeve opening; pin and stitch. Fold a series of knife pleats along base of sleeve, so that sleeve base fits cuff; pin and tack in place.

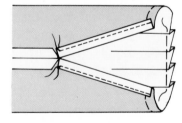

▦ Fold each cuff in half lengthways with right sides together; pin and stitch sides with plain seams. Trim and turn cuff to right side.

▦ Pin one raw edge of cuff to base of each sleeve with right sides together and stitch with plain seam. Turn in remaining raw edge of cuff and pin and topstitch in place.

▦ Place hood side to hood top with right sides together; pin and stitch with plain seams from A to B. Place hood to hood bases with right sides together; pin and stitch with plain seams from C to D. Repeat with hood lining

pieces, and then stitch front facings to edges of hood base lining from E to F.

▦ Fix two eyelets in hood edge at marked positions, following manufacturer's instructions.

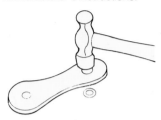

▦ Join hood to jacket at each side, F to E to D to D to E to F with plain seams. Pin hood lining/facing to jacket hood with right sides together; using plain seams, stitch around front edges of jacket and hood, catching in raw front edges of pocket. Trim and turn to inside. Neaten raw edges of facings and handstitch in place around hood. Topstitch around hood to resemble a flat fell seam.

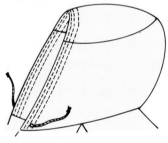

▦ Make a casing by topstitching two rows, 2cm (¾in) and 1.5cm (⅝in) from edges of front hood. Thread cord round casing from eyelet to eyelet. Knot ends.

▦ Fix two eyelets in position through jacket only (not facing) just below seam, 4cm (1½in) from front edges.

▦ Place bias binding around jacket just below waistline to provide a casing for the cord; pin and topstitch in place. Thread cord round casing from eyelet to eyelet. Knot ends.

▦ Turn up lower edges of parka, including facing edges, to form a double 2cm (¾in) hem; pin and topstitch in place.

▦ Fix press stud fasteners down centre front edges and on each cuff, following manufacturer's instructions.

THE SQUARE BAND

Bold squares look great on these ample jackets that are just the job for the whole gang when the weather turns cold. Lumberjack styling with leather buttons and leather-trimmed pockets give these jackets a rugged grown-up look. The lining in brushed cotton makes them all the warmer.

Size: to fit a three-year-old.

MATERIALS

1m (1yd) of 114cm (45in) wide check wool fabric
70cm (¾yd) of 90cm (36in) wide brushed cotton or fine wool for lining
10cm (4in) of 140cm (54in) wide imitation leather
15cm (6in) of 140cm (54in) wide imitation fur

Five 2cm (¾in) diameter imitation leather buttons
Two 1cm (⅜in) diameter imitation leather buttons
Dressmakers' pattern paper
Matching thread

METHOD

▦ Draw up patterns from diagrams. Cut out following cutting instructions.

▦ For pocket piping, cut eight strips of imitation leather, each 13cm × 3cm (5⅛in × 1¼in). For bottom pocket flaps, cut out four pieces of woollen fabric each 13cm × 6.5cm (5⅛in × 2½in). For pocket linings, cut out four pieces of lining fabric each 13cm × 23cm (5⅛in × 9in). Tack a line 1.3cm (½in) below centre across lining to mark position of slit. Mark stitching lines on jacket and lining. Mark slit line on jacket.

▦ Place two pocket flaps with right sides together; pin and stitch both sides and one long edge. Trim and turn to right side.

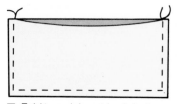

▦ Fold two piping strips in half

lengthways with wrong sides together; pin and tack strips along both sides of slit on stitching lines at each base pocket position, with raw edges facing.

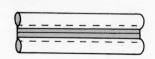

▦ Place flap over top stitching line, with raw edge facing slit, and tack; then place pocket lining over flap, matching stitching lines and with longer side of lining above the slit line. Stitch through all layers along stitching lines and across both ends. Cut along slit line to within 6mm (¼in) of each end; snip into corners.

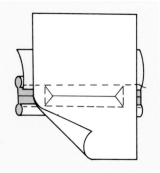

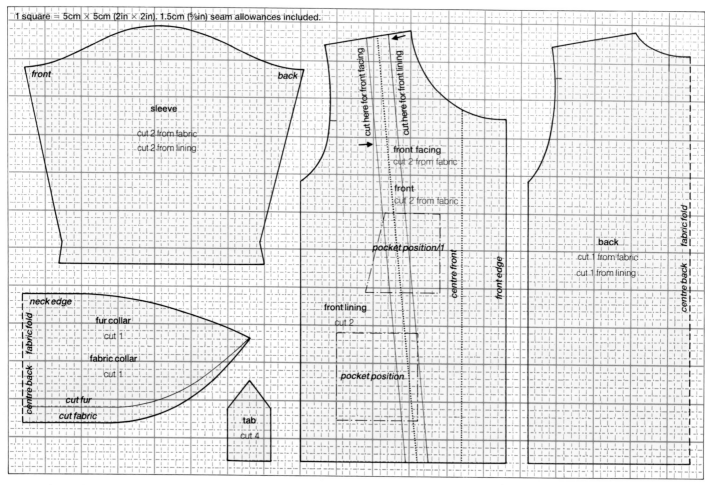

1 square = 5cm × 5cm (2in × 2in). 1.5cm (⅝in) seam allowances included.

▦ Push piping and lining through slit. Form an even piping on right side and topstitch along seam line.

▦ Fold top part of pocket lining over lower part, keeping it free from jacket and flap; pin and stitch to form pocket bag. Trim and neaten.

▦ Make top pockets in the same way, omitting flaps and slanting pocket sides (see photograph).

▦ From imitation leather, cut eight triangles, each with two sides 3cm (1¼in) long, and a 4cm (1½in) long base. Topstitch one at each end of pocket slits.

▦ From imitation leather, cut two strips each 27cm × 1.5cm (10½in × ⅝in). Position a strip across each front at armhole level; pin and topstitch in place.

▦ Place fronts to back with right sides together; pin and stitch shoulder seams. Place sleeves with right side to front/back; pin and stitch in place.

▦ To make up each sleeve tab: place two tab pieces with right sides together; pin and stitch together, leaving short straight edges open. Trim and turn to right side. Topstitch close to outer edge.

▦ Pin each tab on sleeve, with raw edges along side seam, 6cm (2½in) up from wrist.

▦ Fold jacket so that front and back have right sides together; pin and stitch side seams, continuing stitching along underarm seams of sleeves, catching in tabs. Trim and neaten.

▦ Pin and stitch front facings to linings, then make up lining in the same way as jacket, omitting tabs and pockets.

▦ With right sides together, pin and stitch fur collar to neck edge of lining. With right sides together, pin and stitch fabric collar to neck edge of fabric jacket.

▦ To make up three button loops, cut three strips of imitation leather, each 8cm × 1.5cm (3¼in × ⅝in). Fold strips in half lengthways with wrong sides together; topstitch down length close to edge. Fold into loops and pin to left front, 4cm (1½in), 13cm (5⅛in) and 22cm (8¾in) from neck edges; tack.

▦ With right sides together, place lining to jacket. Pin and stitch together from base of right front around to base of left front,

catching in button loops and continuing around collar. Trim and turn to right side. Topstitch front 6mm (¼in) from edges.

▦ Roll outer edge of fabric collar over to front to form a border around fur collar. Topstitch to hold in place.

▦ Push lining sleeves down fabric sleeves, then turn up both hems with raw edges to inside along marked line; pin and topstitch together. Finish base edge of jacket in the same way.

▦ Stitch three large buttons to jacket right front to match loops, and two large buttons on the left side in line with loops.

▦ Fold sleeve tabs on sleeves and stitch ends in place through smaller buttons.

PARTY PURSES

Little girls seem to need an endless supply of purses, bags and cases to hold their favourite trinkets. One of these would make a perfect present. You can draw up pattern pieces to the required size using the diagrams overleaf as a guide, adding 1.5cm (⅝in) seam allowances where necessary.

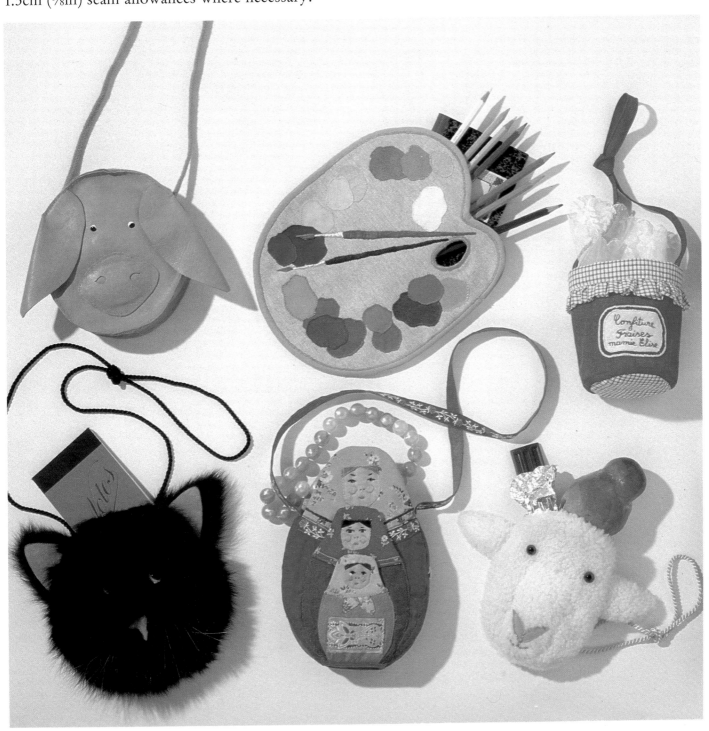

MATERIALS FOR CAT BAG

Size: *15cm (6in) in diameter*
Piece of black fur fabric
40cm × 30cm (16in × 12in)
Oddment of grey felt
Oddment of pink leather
One pair of glass eyes

65cm (26in) of black cord
White nylon thread
20cm (8in) of 90cm (36in) wide
lining fabric
Fabric adhesive
Matching thread

▦ Using diagram as a guide, cut out 2 main sections from fur fabric and 2 from lining. Cut ears from fur fabric and felt. Cut nose from leather.

▦ Fix the glass eyes in bag front at marked positions. Cut whiskers from nylon thread and position ends at marked nose position. Stick nose in place over whiskers; slipstitch in place.

▦ Place ears together in pairs: one grey ear to one black ear with right sides together; pin and

stitch all round, leaving base edges open. Trim and turn to right side. Place to bag front at marked positions. Pin each end of cord strap at marked positions.

▦ Place bag back to bag front with right sides together; pin and stitch together, catching in ears and cord ends and leaving an opening at top edge. Trim and turn to right side.

▦ Make up lining and stitch to bag in the same way as for sheep bag.

MATERIALS FOR RUSSIAN DOLL

Size: *23cm × 15cm (9in × 6in)*
Oddments of plain cotton fabric
in three different colours
Oddments of printed cotton
fabric in three different colours
Oddment of wadding

Embroidery cottons and machine
embroidery threads
Scrap of pink felt
Assortment of braids
Matching thread

▦ Using diagram as guide, cut 4 large doll shapes and 2 each of smaller dolls. Cut shawls from printed fabric and faces from felt. Cut 2 × 5cm (2in) wide gussets.

▦ Place upper bag pieces in position on main doll bag as shown in diagram; pin and stitch.

▦ Position a gusset to each side of 2 main bag pieces with right sides together; pin and stitch.

▦ Embroider the face with straight stitches and French knots, adding small pink felt circles for cheeks. Embroider hands at each side and a plait at the back.

▦ Position a length of braid on each side of bag where upper bag piece ends; pin and stitch in place, adding rows of machine embroidery stitches above the braid.

▦ For the lining, join gusset to main bag pieces as above, leaving an opening in one seam. Place lining to bag with right sides together; pin and stitch around bag top. Trim and turn to right side. Turn in opening; slipstitch to close.

▦ Cut a 65cm (25½in) length of braid for the handle; tuck under raw ends and stitch to each side.

▦ Make up two more dolls with embroidered fronts and printed cotton backs, with a layer of wadding inside.

▦ On the front of the smaller doll, position a length of embroidered ribbon to form a pocket; stitch base and sides.

▦ Place dolls one on top of the other; stitch base and sides, leaving openings at the top, so that they form pockets.

MATERIALS FOR PIGGY

Size: 17cm (6¾in) in diameter
Piece of pink leather 30cm ×
70cm (12in × 28in)

Plastic or glass eyes
13cm (5in) zip
Suitable filling and thread

METHOD

▦ Draw up pattern using diagram as a guide. Cut out 2 main sections, 4 ears and 1 muzzle.

▦ Cut out a 7.5cm (3in) wide gusset to fit all round bag front and back. Stitch gusset ends together to form a ring. Cut an 11cm (4⅜in) long slit centrally in gusset. Position zip in slit; stitch in place.

▦ On bag front, fix eyes at positions marked. Cut out nostril shapes from muzzle. Position muzzle to bag front; topstitch in place.

▦ Place gusset to bag front with zip placed at centre top; topstitch in place. Make a 2cm (¾in) slit across gusset on each side of zip.

▦ Cut a strap 65cm × 2cm (26in × ¾in) from leather. Insert ends through slits at sides of zip and topstitch in place. Open zip. Topstitch bag back to opposite side of gusset.

▦ Place ears in pairs with wrong sides together; topstitch, adding a small amount of filling inside each one. Place ears to sides of bag and topstitch in place.

Imitate the wooden Russian dolls with embroidered clothes and features. The graduating size of the dolls is effectively reproduced by the two doll pockets.

A pink leather pig is just the answer for carrying around all the valuables. The zip opening is set into the gusset top and the shoulder strap ends slot in at each side before being stitched in place, to give practicality to a fun idea.

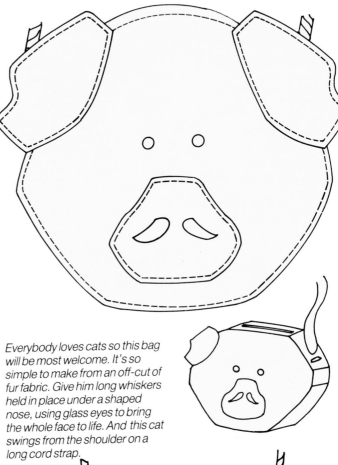

Everybody loves cats so this bag will be most welcome. It's so simple to make from an off-cut of fur fabric. Give him long whiskers held in place under a shaped nose, using glass eyes to bring the whole face to life. And this cat swings from the shoulder on a long cord strap.

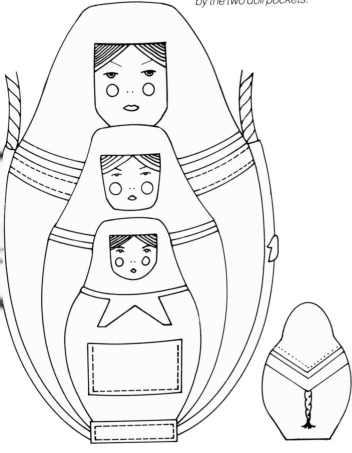

MATERIALS FOR JAM POT

Size: *10cm × 15cm (4in × 6in)*
50cm (⅝yd) of 90cm (36in) wide gingham
2.15m (2½yd) of 2cm (¾in) wide petersham ribbon

Small piece of wadding
Oddment of 2.5cm (1in) wide bias binding
Embroidery cotton
Matching thread

METHOD

▦ Using diagram as a guide, cut out 2 main sections, one 2cm (¾in) deeper than the other from gingham and one from wadding.

▦ Position lengths of petersham ribbon side by side to cover one bag piece; pin and topstitch in place. With right sides together, pin and stitch side seam.

❑ Cut out a circle of gingham to fit base. Place base to sides with wrong sides together; pin and stitch around base. Trim.

▦ Fold bias binding over raw edges of base; pin and topstitch in place.

▦ Overlap side edges of wadding piece; pin and stitch together. Cut out and stitch a wadding base to wadding sides. Place inside bag.

▦ Pin and stitch lining together in the same way.

▦ Cut a 5cm (2in) wide strip of gingham 1½ times the circumference of the bag; pin and stitch short ends together, to form a ring. Turn under a double 6mm (¼in) hem; pin and stitch. Work a row of gathering stitches along opposite edge. Pull up gathers evenly and pin to top edge of ribboned bag, with wrong sides together 1.3cm (½in) down from edge; stitch in place.

▦ Place lining inside bag, with wrong sides together; turn lining over at top edge to form a 2cm (¾in) wide band, then turn under raw edge; pin and slipstitch.

▦ Embroider lettering onto the label and pin it to the front of the bag. Stitch in place with buttonhole stitch.

▦ For handle, cut a 65cm (25½in) strip of ribbon. Fold in half lengthways; pin and topstitch all round. Place to each side of bag; stitch in place.

A pot of jam can hide a variety of secrets. Lengths of ribbon provide the pot and long shoulder strap, while the top has a cheerful gingham cover. Then embroider a name on the label at the front.

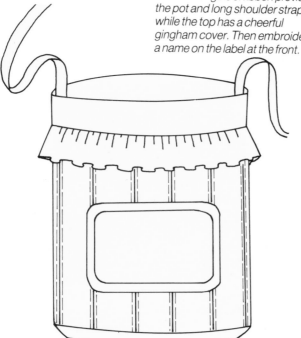

MATERIALS FOR SHEEP BAG

Size: 17cm × 13cm (6¾in × 5¼in)
Piece of white fur fabric 40cm × 20cm (16in × 8in)
Oddment of pink leather
65cm (25½in) pink cord

20cm (8in) of 90cm (36in) wide lining fabric
One pair of glass eyes
Suitable filling
Embroidery cotton
Matching thread

METHOD

▦ Using diagram as guide, cut 2 main sections, 4 ears and muzzle from fur fabric and 2 lining sections. Cut nose from leather.
▦ Place nose to muzzle; pin and topstitch in place. Embroider mouth in grey. Place muzzle to front of bag; pin and slipstitch in place, adding a small amount of filling.
▦ Fix glass eyes in place above muzzle. Place two ears with right sides together; pin and stitch, leaving base edges open. Trim and turn to right side. Add a little filling and pin in position on bag front.

▦ Place bag back to bag front with right sides together; pin and stitch, catching in ears, and leaving top edge open. Trim and turn to right side.
▦ For lining, place back to front with right sides together; pin and stitch, leaving top edge free and an opening in one side.
▦ Pin ends of cord to either side of head (see photograph).
▦ Place lining to bag with right sides together; pin and stitch together around top, catching in cord ends. Trim and turn to right side. Turn in opening edges; pin and slipstitch together to close. Push lining down inside bag.

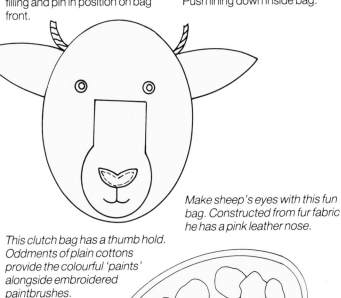

Make sheep's eyes with this fun bag. Constructed from fur fabric he has a pink leather nose.

This clutch bag has a thumb hold. Oddments of plain cottons provide the colourful 'paints' alongside embroidered paintbrushes.

MATERIALS FOR ARTIST'S PALETTE

Size: 25cm × 21cm (10in × 8¼in)
50cm (⅝yd) of 90cm (36in) wide canvas
Oddments of cotton poplin fabric

Bonding fabric
1.5m (1⅝yd) of 1.3cm (½in) wide bias binding
Embroidery cottons
Matching thread

METHOD

▦ Using diagram as a guide, cut out 4 main sections. Mark position for hole.
▦ Place back pieces with wrong sides together; pin and tack. Repeat with front pieces.
▦ On bag front and back, cut out marked hole, and buttonhole stitch around the outer edge.
▦ Iron oddments of different coloured fabrics to one side of bonding fabric.

▦ Cut out each paint shape. Position on bag front and press in place. Stitch all round. Embroider paintbrushes.
▦ Fold bias binding over the outer edges of bag fronts; pin and topstitch in place. Bind backs in same way.
▦ Place back and front bag pieces with wrong sides together; pin and stitch together, following previous stitching lines and leaving top edge open.

VERSATILE COLLARS

Smart little collars for a precious baby. They are quickly made – just cut out two layers of fine-quality cotton following the patterns shown and finish the inside neck edge with bias binding.

MATERIALS

PLAIN COLLARS
20cm (8in) of 90cm (36in) wide fabric
Oddment of iron-on interfacing
One 1.5cm (⅝in) diameter button
Matching thread

PLEATED COLLAR
20cm (8in) of 90cm (36in) wide printed cotton fabric
One 1.5cm (⅝in) diameter button
Matching thread

BRODERIE ANGLAISE TOP
30cm (⅓yd) of 90cm (36in) wide broderie anglaise
2m (2⅛yd) of 1.3cm (½in) wide bias binding
One 1.5cm (⅝in) diameter button
Matching thread

METHOD

Plain collar

▦ Draw up the pattern from the diagram following the lines for the desired edge. Cut out twice from fabric, adding a 1.5cm (⅝in) seam allowance all round; cut out once from iron-on interfacing. Position interfacing shiny-side down centrally on wrong side of one collar piece; press in place.

▦ Place collar pieces with right sides together; pin and stitch round edge of interfacing, leaving an opening at one back edge. Trim and turn to the right side. Turn in seam allowance along open back edge; slipstitch to close.

▦ Work a buttonloop on the right-hand side of the back collar. Stitch a button to the left-hand side of the collar to correspond.

Pleated collar

▦ Cut a strip of fabric 86cm × 7.5cm (34½in × 3in). Turn under a 1.5cm (⅝in) hem, then tuck under raw edge for 6mm (¼in); pin and hem in place.

▦ Fold collar up into 6mm (¼in) knife pleats; pin and tack.

▦ Cut a 2.5cm (1in) wide strip of self-fabric on the bias the length of the neck edge. Place one edge of bias strip to right side of pleated collar; pin and stitch. Fold strip to wrong side over raw edge of collar, then tuck under raw

ends; pin and slipstitch in place over previous stitches.

▦ Fasten the collar at the back edge with button loop and button, as for previous collar.

Broderie Anglaise top

▦ Draw up the pattern from the diagram. Cut out once from fabric adding 1.3cm (½in) all round outer edge and 1.5cm (⅝in) round neck edge.

▦ Turn under a double 6mm (¼in) wide hem all round the outer edge. Pin and stitch in place, folding neat corners.

▦ Unfold bias binding and place one edge with right side to neck edge of collar; pin and stitch. Turn binding to wrong side, then tuck under raw ends; pin and slipstitch remaining edge in place.

▦ Fasten the collar at the back edge with buttonloop and button, as for previous collars.

▦ To make up ties, cut four 30cm (12in) pieces of binding. Fold each piece in half lengthways, then tuck in raw ends; pin and topstitch all round. Stitch to each corner.

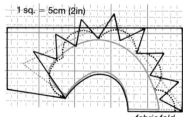

1 sq. = 5cm (2in)

fabric fold

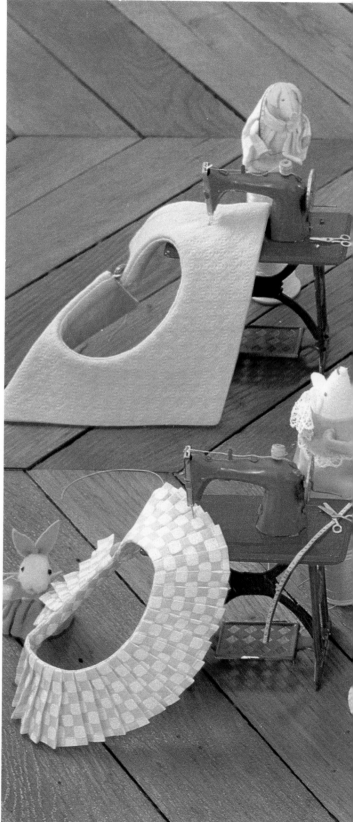

APPLIQUE TRICKS

What child doesn't love animals with a passion? One – if not all – of these creatures will be sure to be an instant success. Transform classic clothes with personal favourites: rabbits, mice, puppies and cats can all be cut out of scraps of fabric and appliquéd wherever you choose – follow the patterns and surprise them peeking out of pockets.

MATERIALS

CAT AND MOUSE
Tracing paper
Oddments of grey, white, green and printed fabric
One skein of DMC embroidery silk in each of the following colours: **white, black** *310,* **grey** *415,* **grey** *414,* **red** *666,* **green** *907,* **blue** *996,* **pink** *3689,* **pink** *760 and* **dark brown** *433*
Matching thread

DOGS
Tracing paper
Oddments of dark brown, black, grey and beige fabric
One skein of DMC embroidery silk in each of the following colours: **white, black** *310,* **green** *907,* **blue** *518,* **pink** *3689 and* **grey** *414*
Matching thread

RABBITS
Tracing paper
Oddments of dark brown, black, grey and beige fabric
One skein of DMC embroidery silk in each of the following colours: **white, grey** *413,* **grey** *415,* **pink** *754,* **green** *704,* **blue** *518,* **orange** *741 and* **orange** *970*
Matching thread

METHOD

▦ Trace off each section of the desired motif and cut out. Pin the motif patterns to the right side of the chosen fabrics (see photograph) and mark around the outer edge, and then mark an allowance of 3mm (⅛in) all round each shape. Cut out outside the marked areas.
▦ Staystitch, with small stitches, all round the motif pieces, just outside the inner marked line. Cut out each piece along outer marked line, cutting into curves and corners and across points.
▦ Turn under allowance all round each piece and tack.
▦ Place motif pieces on background, fitting them together by slightly overlapping the edges; pin and tack. Slipstitch each piece in place by hand.
▦ Embroider the remaining parts of the animals, using straight stitch, satin stitch and stem stitch. Halve the embroidery skein when stitching muzzle, eyes, whiskers and claws.

Hopping, skipping or just jumping, these little animals will bring the plainest of garments to life – give them textured fabric bodies and embroider their mischievous features.

Page	Acknowledgments (Photographer/Stylist)
1	Gilles de Chabaneix/Catherine de Chabaneix
4	Jacques Dirand/Anne Luntz
9	Jacques Dirand/Yveline Hollier-Larousse
11	Marcel Duffas/Caroline Lebeau
15,17	Gilles de Chabaneix/Catherine de Chabaneix
19,21	Jerome Tisné/Isabelle Garçon
23,24,25	Gilles de Chabaneix/Marion Faver
27,28,31,32	Gilles de Chabaneix/Catherine de Chabaneix
34	Gilles de Chabaneix/Catherine de Chabaneix
36	Jerome Tisné/Caroline Lebeau
39,40	Gilles de Chabaneix/Catherine de Chabaneix
42	Daniel Burgi/Anne Luntz
43,45	Jerome Tisné/Isabelle Garçon
47,49	Jacques Dirand/Anne Luntz
50,51,53,54	Daniel Burgi/Isabelle Garçon
55,56,57	Gilles de Chabaneix/Catherine de Chabaneix
58	Gilles de Chabaneix/Catherine de Chabaneix
61,64,65	Bernard Maltaverne/Caroline Lebeau
67	Gilles de Chabaneix/Catherine de Chabaneix
69,70,72,73	Alex Bianchi/Jannick Schoumacher
75	Gilles de Chabaneix/Catherine de Chabaneix
76,77,78,79	Jerome Tisné/Isabelle Garçon